Viva World Cup!

Tales from the Greatest Football Show on Earth

Nick Brownlee

PORTICO

First published in the United Kingdom in 2014 by
Portico
10 Southcombe Street
London
W14 0RA

An imprint of Anova Books Company Ltd.

ISBN 978 1 909396 72 2

A CIP catalogue record for this book is available from the British Library.

10 9 8 7 6 5 4 3 2 1

Illustrations by Gary Weston
Printed and bound by Bookwell, Finland

This book can be ordered direct from the publisher at
www.anovabooks.com

FOREWORD

The last time the World Cup was held in Brazil, in 1950, only thirteen teams took part. England flew there: the flight took 31 hours, stopping in Paris, Lisbon, Dakar and Recife, and when the squad landed in Rio de Janeiro, three men in gas masks stepped onto the plane and sprayed everyone on board with pesticide.

Quite how today's pampered superstars would put up with such an ordeal is a matter for debate. Nearly 65 years after Stanley Matthews, Stan Mortensen, Jackie Milburn and co ran onto the pitch for their opening game against Chile, the game and its players have changed beyond all recognition.

In terms of sheer scale, the event is now a global behemoth. This year's finals will feature 32 teams from as far afield as South Korea and Ivory Coast, has cost upwards of £8 billion to stage, and will be watched by around half the world's population. Yet the beauty of the World Cup – or the FIFA World Cup as we must now call it – is that despite the rampant bite of commercialism and globalisation, some things will never change about the great old tournament. On the pitch there will be heroes and villains, unheralded headliners and faded superstars, brilliant goals, outstanding saves, unbelievable howlers, edge-of-the-seat excitement and mind-numbing boredom. Great teams will crash out, underdogs will defy the odds. And on July 13, after four weeks of thrills and spills, tears and joy, two sides will line up in front of 80,000 spectators to compete for football's ultimate trophy. It is for these reasons that, every four years, we say Viva World Cup and settle down to watch the greatest show on earth.

This book celebrates the players and teams who have made their mark on the history of the tournament, but the aim has been to delve behind the headlines, shining a spotlight on those lesser-known characters and incidents that are as much a part of World Cup folklore as the superstars and the great matches. I hope you enjoy reading about them as much as I enjoyed writing this book.

Nick Brownlee
Cumbria, February 2014

IN THE BEGINNING

The first World Cup match took place on a warm Sunday afternoon on 13 July 1930 in the Pocitos suburb of Montevideo, the capital city of Uruguay. Just over 1,000 people watched France's Lucien Laurent score the competition's first goal with a powerful shot after nineteen minutes, then saw the French romp to a convincing 4–1 victory over Mexico. This was despite the European team losing goalkeeper Alex Thepot after just 10 minutes, having been kicked on the jaw. Captain of France that day was Alex Villaplane, who 14 years later would be executed by his fellow countrymen for collaborating with the Nazis.

PENALTY FIRST

The semi-final between France and West Germany in 1982 was the first World Cup match to be decided by a penalty shoot-out. Alain Giresse, the French midfielder, stepped up to take the first kick — and was a relieved man when goalkeeper Harald Schumacher went the wrong way. Unfortunately for Giresse, the rest of his teammates weren't so accurate, and France crashed out of the competition 5–4.

ON, AND VERY NEARLY OFF

The fastest yellow card given to a substitute in a World Cup finals match was to South Korea's Cha Doo-Ri, who was booked just 20 seconds after coming on in the match against Poland in 2002.

ONLY IN JAPAN

The Kobe stadium in Japan, used during the 2002 World Cup to stage matches in Group F among others, had a unique computer system used to control the length and growth-rate of the grass on the pitch.

BLACKOUT IN BANGLADESH

Such was the global allure of the 1998 World Cup, impoverished districts of Bangladesh had four nights of blackouts due to a surge in power consumption as millions of people tuned in to watch football coverage from France.

DROWNING THEIR SORROWS

After seeing their side lose 3–0 to unfancied Morocco at the 1998 World Cup, around 8,000 travelling Scotland fans drowned their sorrows by drinking 125,000 litres of beer between them. Several bars in St Etienne had to close after the barrels ran dry.

IN THE NAME OF THE FATHER

Who needs the pub? FIFA granted German Evangelical churches the rights to screen all World Cup 2006 matches free of charge. 'Football is a vital part of life', said Bishop Wolfgang Huber of the Evangelical Church. Amen to that.

AN UNWELCOME RECORD

In 2002, Hakan Unsal of Turkey became the 100th player to be sent off during the World Cup finals.

THE MISSING 'V'

Milko Gaidarski (1970) and Petar Mikhtarski (1994) are the only two Bulgarian World Cup players out of 154 not to have the letter 'v' at the end of their names.

WORLD CUP MASCOTS

Tournament	Mascot	Description
England 1966	World Cup Willie	A lion wearing a Union Jack jersey.
Mexico 1970	Juanito	A Mexican boy wearing a sombrero.
West Germany 1974	Tip and Tap	Two boys in West German shirts.
Argentina 1978	Gauchito	A boy in a gaucho hat.
Spain 1982	Naranjito	A smiling orange.
Mexico 1986	Pique	A chilli pepper.
Italy 1990	Ciao	A figure made of coloured blocks.
USA 1994	Striker	A cartoon dog.
France 1998	Footix	A cockerel.
Japan/S. Korea 2002	Kaz, Ato and Nik	Three manga-style cartoon characters.
Germany 2006	Goleo VI and Pille	A large lion in a German football top, accompanied by his friend, a talking football.
South Africa 2010	Zakumi	A green-haired leopard.
Brazil 2014	Fuleco	A three-banded armadillo.

Ciao
Italy 1990

World Cup Willy
England 1966

Footix
France 1998

Naranjito
Spain 1982

Goleo VI & Pille
Germany 2006

MYANMAR MISERY

Myanmar, known as Burma until 1989, finished second in the 1968 Asian Cup. But their record in the World Cup is, well, non-existent. Between 1930 and 1938 they did not enter, while in 1950 they were invited to enter but withdrew. From 1954–90 they did not enter. In 1994 they entered but withdrew without playing a match. In 1998 they did not enter, and in 2002 they were entered but once again withdrew. In 2006, FIFA's patience snapped and Myanmar were banned from even entering the tournament. In seventeen tournaments they are the only national side registered with FIFA not to play a single World Cup qualifier.

GREAT GAMES: France 1–1 Brazil (4–3 after penalties), 1986

A quarter-final in Guadalajara in which a host of brilliant but ageing players realised that this could well be their last hurrah on the world stage and performed accordingly. Careca scored after 17 minutes for Brazil, but Platini levelled 4 minutes before half time. In the shoot-out, Socrates, Platini and Cesar all missed as France scraped through 4–3. But in many ways the score was unimportant. What caught the eye were the likes of Socrates, Platini, Rocheteau, Zico and Junior playing out of their skins for the last time, and the overwhelming feeling among millions of viewers that, whatever the result, this was the end of a golden era of World Cup football.

HAVELANGE SPLASHES OUT

Joao Havelange, the former President of FIFA, was not much of a footballer by all accounts. However, as a young man he represented Brazil in swimming at the 1936 Berlin Olympics and in water polo at the 1952 Games in Helsinki.

RONALDO'S ILLNESS

Just what was wrong with Ronaldo before the 1998 World Cup final? It is a mystery that provided the major talking point of the tournament, even more than France's 3–0 win. The drama began on the day of the match, when the prolific striker was sensationally left out of the starting eleven. The reason given was an unspecified illness – which began a frenzy of speculation about what had happened. Rumours varied from epileptic fits to poisoning. Then, with barely an hour to go before kickoff, Ronaldo was back in the team, creating even more gossip. Had his sponsors insisted that he played? Was he really ill in the first place? Was coach Mario Zagallo playing mind games with the French? Ronaldo played, but was woefully out of sorts. He missed the sort of chances he would normally be expected to gobble up as France cruised to victory. Later Ronaldo explained that even he didn't know what was wrong with him, except that he felt 'bad'. Four years later he was back to his best, scoring both goals in Brazil's 2–0 final win over Germany. But the puzzle remains about 1998 and the illness that conveniently sidelined Brazil's most influential player on the eve of the World Cup final.

ROBSON'S CHOICE

Often it is the Fates and not the manager's selections which can make or break the fortunes of a team competing in the World Cup. So it was with England in 1986. Bobby Robson's men made a disastrous start to their Mexican campaign, losing to Portugal and scraping a goalless draw against little Morocco. In their final game they were up against Poland, and anything less than a draw would see them on the first flight back to Blighty. Robson's selections had been roundly criticised, but now the Fates stepped in. In the Morocco match, England lost both skipper Bryan Robson (dislocated collarbone) and midfielder Ray Wilkins (sent off). Without what were assumed to be his two most influential players and with the shape of his team unbalanced, Robson was forced to play little Peter Beardsley as a foil for striker Gary Lineker. Right from the first whistle it was clear that here was a match made in heaven.

Beardsley was instrumental in all three of Lineker's first-half goals and would go on to score himself in the next match, a convincing 3–0 win against Paraguay. Lineker scored two this time, putting him on course for a Golden Boot and England for a quarter-final spot – neither of which seemed possible before the Fates robbed Robson of his captain and his midfield general.

SAME COUNTRY, DIFFERENT NAME

Look back through the World Cup annals and there are a number of teams who have appeared in qualifiers and the finals who at first glance seem to have disappeared off the map. That's because, whether because of political or social change, they have changed their names to reappear with a new name. These countries include:

- ⚽ Benin who, as Dahomey, attempted to qualify in 1974
- ⚽ Burkina Faso, known as Upper Volta in 1978
- ⚽ Democratic Republic of Congo, who appeared as Zaire from 1970 to 1998
- ⚽ Czech Republic and Slovakia, who were together as Czechoslovakia from 1934 until 1994; they split in 1993 and completed the 1994 qualifiers as RCS – Representation of Czechs and Slovaks
- ⚽ Germany, also known as Saarland in 1954 and German Democratic Republic, or West Germany, from 1958 until 1990 before uniting back again
- ⚽ Indonesia, who made a fleeting appearance in the finals as the Dutch East Indies in 1938
- ⚽ Republic of Ireland, who attempted to qualify as Irish Free States in 1934 and 1938
- ⚽ Israel, known as Palestine in 1934 and 1938
- ⚽ Myanmar, who were Burma in 1950
- ⚽ Netherlands Antilles, who were Curaçao in 1958
- ⚽ Russia and Ukraine, who were the USSR from 1958 until 1994
- ⚽ Sri Lanka, who made a bid for World Cup glory as Ceylon in 1974

⚽ Surinam, who were Dutch Guyana in 1938, 1962, 1966, 1970 and 1974
⚽ Vietnam SR, who entered as South Vietnam in 1974 and 1978
⚽ Yemen, who entered as both North Yemen and South Yemen in 1974 and 1978
⚽ Serbia and Montenegro, who were known as The Kingdom of Serbia and Montenegro in 1930

REFUSED ENTRY

FIFA may give the impression that any nation can enter the World Cup, but in fact they have refused entry to sixteen teams since the tournament began in 1930. In all, 77 countries have withdrawn, been disqualified, suspended, excluded or expelled in seventeen World Cups.

The teams to be refused entry are:

Albania...1970
Belize 1990
Bolivia...1954
French Congo (Congo) 1966
Zaire (Democratic Republic of Congo) 1970
Costa Rica 1954
Cuba .... 1954 & 1970
Ethiopia...1957
Guatemala 1966
Guinea...1970
Iceland...1954
Korean Republic 1958
Mauritius..1990
Mozambique 1990
Spain...1938
Vietnam SR 1954

SECOND CHANCE SPURNED

Sierra Leone lost to Burundi in the first qualifying round of the 1958 World Cup and were therefore eliminated from the competition. Then war broke out in Burundi, which meant they had no choice but to withdraw. FIFA decided that Sierra Leone should therefore be reinstated, but domestic problems meant that they couldn't fulfil their fixtures. They therefore became the only country to be eliminated twice from the same World Cup.

THE WORLD OF FIFA

Six governing bodies make up the Federation of International Football Associations (FIFA). They are:
- ⚽ UEFA (Union of European Football Associations)
- ⚽ CAF (Confederation of African Football)
- ⚽ CONCACAF (Confederation of North, Central American and Caribbean Association Football)
- ⚽ CONMEBOL (Confederation of South American Football)
- ⚽ OFC (Oceania Football Confederation)
- ⚽ AFC (Asian Football Confederation)

A GLOBAL MEDIA EVENT

The 2010 World Cup was shown in every country and territory on the planet, including Antarctica and the Arctic Circle, generating record-breaking viewing figures of over 3.2 billion people – or 46.4 per cent of the global population. It was covered by nearly 4,000 accredited journalists and 5,000 TV and radio crews. It was also the first World Cup to be broadcast fully in High Definition, although that proved to be a curse for England fans who missed Steven Gerrard's opening goal against the USA due to a glitch which briefly cut UK transmission at the vital moment, replacing it instead with a commercial.

JABULANIS AND BRAZUCAS

In Zulu the word means 'Rejoice'. But the Adidas Jabulani ball, introduced for the 2010 World Cup, brought little cheer to the teams who had to play with it. Despite being designed in conjunction with scientists from Loughborough University in the UK to be perfectly aerodynamic, the ball soon proved to have a life of its own. Goalkeepers were especially critical: according to England's reserve keeper Joe Hart, '... the balls have been doing anything but staying in my gloves', sentiments echoed by the likes of Gianluigi Buffon of Italy and Brazil's Julio Cesar, who compared it to a 'supermarket' football. The furore has not affected Adidas, who were once again chosen by FIFA to design the ball for the 2014 tournament in Brazil. The Brazuca – the name was chosen by public vote, with over one million Brazilians taking part – is supposed to be even more aerodynamic than the Jabulani, and the manufacturer claims it will be the 'most colourful' ball ever used in the World Cup.

FRENCH REVOLUTION

Despite a team containing such luminaries as Hugo Lloris, Franck Ribery, Nicolas Anelka and Patrice Evra, the 2010 World Cup was to prove a complete and utter disaster for France. Not only did they fail to win a game, drawing against Uruguay while losing to Mexico and South Africa, the squad staged a mutiny against coach Raymond Domenech before the decisive final game after he sent Anelka home. The fallout back home was brutal; Domenech was fired, while many of the mutineers were dropped from the national side.

VIVA LA VUVUZELA?

If the football was at times forgettable at South Africa 2010 then the vuvuzela most certainly wasn't. This trumpet-shaped plastic instrument and its ubiquitous drone came to define the tournament from the very first kickoff, with thousands of them being blown in unison from the packed stands. The reaction at first was one of quizzical amusement – but this soon turned to irritation, especially among foreign broadcasters who found themselves inundated with complaints from their viewers about the noise. There were even claims that the incessant buzzing was affecting the players' ability to perform, although strangely the better teams didn't seem too bothered. Calls for a blanket vuvuzela ban were gleefully ignored by the crowd, and eventually the TV companies were obliged to use noise-masking technology to deaden the sound for their transmissions.

BAFANA MAGIC

Few people outside South Africa had ever heard of Siphiwe Tshabalala before the opening game of the 2010 World Cup. Indeed, until 55 minutes into the match against Mexico, the Kaizer Chiefs midfielder had remained largely anonymous. Then came the moment of magic: Kagiso Dikgacoi stroked a perfect 40-yard pass from inside the centre circle to allow Tshabalala to run behind the Mexican defence, and after taking a single touch the winger's left-foot finish flew unstoppably past Oscar Pérez and into his top-left corner. The celebrations were wild and deafening; Bafana Bafana had opened their World Cup account in spectacular style and South Africa 2010 was off and running.

MADIBA MAKES AN APPEARANCE

In 1995 Nelson Mandela had presented the rugby union World Cup trophy to victorious Springbok captain Francois Pienaar in a moment rich in symbolism for the South African nation. Fifteen years later, however, it was uncertain whether the almost 92-year-old would appear at the final of the football World Cup, having pulled out of the opening ceremony after the death of his great-granddaughter in a car accident hours before and suffering from increasing ill health. The world need not have worried: wrapped against the winter cold, the anti-apartheid hero was shuttled onto the pitch at Soccer City, Johannesburg, on a golf cart and, beaming from ear to ear, waved to the ecstatic 85,000 spectators.

CLAMOUR FOR SAMBA

The fact that the 2014 World Cup would be held in Brazil was never in doubt from the moment FIFA announced its decision to stage the tournament in South America for the first time since Argentina in 1978. But, FIFA being FIFA, the Brazilian Soccer Federation (CBF) was still required to jump through the necessary hoops before it was given the nod. In July 2007, therefore, CBF president Ricardo Teixeira submitted a vast, 900-page dossier detailing the Brazilian bid. Three months later, the bid was accepted and Brazil allowed to run uncontested for the position of World Cup hosts for the first time since 1950, having won the tournament five times on foreign soil.

BETTER LATE THAN NEVER

At the age of 71, German-born Otto Rehhagel was the oldest coach ever to attend a World Cup when he coached Greece in South Africa in 2010. Amazingly it was his first tournament, as either manager or player. Back home in Germany, Rehhagel was the first person, as player and as manager, to have participated in more than 1,000 Bundesliga matches (an achievement since matched by Jupp Heynckes). This also explains his nickname: 'Kind der Bundesliga' (child of the Bundesliga).

FRENCH FANCY

The 1998 World Cup final between France and Brazil was the first ever to be contested between the hosts and the defending world champions.

SENEGAL STUNNER

As World Cup shocks go, this one was seismic. The first game of the 2002 World Cup pitched reigning champions France against the unknowns of Senegal. Unknown, that is, until the 29th minute when, following a cross by El Hadji Diouf, midfielder Papa Bouba Diop forced the ball into the back of the net from close range. France, with the likes of Thierry Henry and Marcel Desailly in their team, were lousy and never looked like equalising. In fact, they failed to perform in their other games and went out in the group stage without scoring a goal. Senegal, in their first ever World Cup finals, remained sanguine about their sensational win. 'Before the game we all believe we can make a good result,' said midfielder Salif Diao. 'We won the game because we played better.'

NAREY WILL WE SEE THE LIKE AGAIN

In 1982, Brazil produced some sumptuous long-range goals that even today take the breath away. But ironically one of the very best goals of the competition was scored against Brazil and, of all people, by a Scotland defender. Just eighteen minutes had gone of the Group 6 match in Seville when David Narey received the ball midway inside the Brazil half, ran forward and then unleashed a simply unstoppable shot which flew into the net past the helpless Waldir Peres. It was a goal which stunned the Brazilians for precisely fifteen minutes, until Zico equalised. Three more goals followed as Scotland's game collapsed.

THE ART OF BEING A STRIKER

'The big thing is, everybody says it's being in the right place at the right time. But it's more than that, it's being in the right place all the time. Because if I make twenty runs to the near post and each time I lose my defender, and nineteen times the ball goes over my head or behind me – then one time I'm three yards out, the ball comes to the right place and I tap it in – then people say, right place, right time. And I was there all the time.' – England's Gary Lineker, winner of the Golden Boot in 1986.

DEFENCE, THE BEST FORM OF ATTACK

In 1990 Cameroon delighted the world with their plucky displays of attacking football, and very nearly went all the way to the semi-final. In the euphoria it was easy to forget that, when required, the Africans could be brutally pragmatic. In their opening match against Argentina they won the game 1–0, but also perpetrated one of the most cynical and over-the-top fouls ever seen in World Cup history in order to preserve their lead. With just a few minutes to go, Claudio Caniggia, Argentina's rangy, long-haired centre-forward burst clear from halfway and set off towards goal. Almost immediately one of the Cameroon defenders raced in with a challenge which, had Caniggia not somehow hurdled it, would have surely broken his legs. Still bearing down on goal, Caniggia was finally felled by Benjamin Massing, who executed a waist-high flying body check which almost knocked the striker into the third row of the stand. Needless to say Massing was sent for an early bath – the second Cameroon player to be sent off that day for fouls on Caniggia.

OPERA BUFFS

Wary of their reputation as global hooligans, FIFA decided to keep England fans as far away from the rest of Italia '90 as possible by confining them to the island of Sardinia for the first round of matches. In an effort to prove them wrong, a group of England fans made a point of soaking up the culture by going to see a performance of Verdi's opera *Aida* in Cagliari. The verdict? 'Some nice tunes, but the intervals were too long!' one fan complained.

DINING IN REVERSE

In a bid to relieve the boredom between matches, in 1990 England's Terry Butcher and Chris Woods went to a restaurant in Cagliari with their smart Umbro tracksuits inside out. They then proceeded to order coffee, dessert, a main course and then finish up with a starter. They must have been very bored indeed.

IT'S A LINEKER!

During Beirut hostage John McCarthy's captivity, Gary Lineker scored six goals for England at Mexico '86. According to McCarthy, who was allowed to listen to coverage on the radio while chained to a radiator, this led him for a while to think 'Lineker' was Arabic for 'goal'.

KEANE VS MCCARTHY

Irish eyes weren't smiling in the build-up to the 2002 World Cup following the mother of all rows between the Republic's manager Mick McCarthy and his star player and captain Roy Keane. Annoyed by what he regarded as sub-standard training facilities, Keane's frustration boiled over at a team meeting on the eve of their first game. Most of what was said is unprintable, but the gist was that Keane did not regard McCarthy as a good manager. McCarthy reacted by sending Keane home. Despite a concerted campaign to have him reinstated, in which even the Taoiseach (Prime Minister) Bertie Ahern tried to mediate, Keane did not play for Ireland again under McCarthy. Indeed McCarthy stated publicly that if Keane returned he would quit.

A–Z OF WORLD CUP GREATS

ADEMIR (Brazil, b. 1922 d. 1998) Considered one of Brazil's greatest ever strikers, and a precursor to legends Pelé and Zico, Ademir scored nine goals as the host nation blazed its way through the 1950 finals, hitting four in a 7–1 win over third-placed Sweden and two in a 6–1 demolition of Spain in the final group phase.
Tournament 1950 **Games** 6 **Goals** 9

BECKENBAUER, FRANZ (West Germany, b. 1945) Known universally as *der Kaiser* because of his elegant style and leadership qualities, Beckenbauer virtually invented the art of creative defending, maturing from a solid midfielder to an attacking sweeper in a long and illustrious career. He played in three World Cups, losing to England in 1966, enduring a frustrating shoulder injury in 1970, and finally, as captain, lifting the trophy on home soil in 1974. Later he would become coach of the national side, leading them to the final in 1986 and becoming the second man, after Mario Zagallo, to both play in and coach a World Cup-winning team in 1990. He headed the bid to have Germany selected as hosts of the 2006 World Cup, and was head of the organising committee.

Tournaments 1966, 1970, 1974 **Games** 18 **Goals** 5

CUBILLAS, TEOFILO (Peru, b. 1949) One of the most prolific goalscorers in World Cup history, Teofilo Cubillas's ten goals were all the more remarkable considering they were scored in two tournaments eight years apart, and for a team which were generally considered rank outsiders but consistently rewrote the form book. His first tournament was in 1970 when he bagged five goals and helped Peru to the quarter-finals. In 1978, he scored five more – including two against Scotland – which propelled his side to the second stage. Cubillas was back, aged 32, in 1982, but age and a poor side were against him and he failed to score.

Tournaments 1970, 1978, 1982 **Games** 13 **Goals** 10

DUNGA (Brazil, b. 1963) Never as flamboyant as his teammates, Dunga was nevertheless the mainstay of three Brazilian World Cup sides, and skippered the side which won the 1994 World Cup and reached the final in 1998. An excellent defensive midfielder, he brought much-needed solidity to sides full of gifted attacking individuals such as Romario, Ronaldo and Ronaldinho. Although not a noted goalscorer, Dunga bagged the penalty that secured victory in the 1994 shoot-out. Unfortunately, his nickname means 'Dopey' in Portuguese.

Tournaments 1990, 1994, 1998 **Games** 18 **Goals** 0 (2 in penalty shoot-outs)

EUSEBIO (Portugal, b. 1942) You don't have to be a World Cup winner to be a World Cup star. Eusebio – known as the Black Pearl – dominated the 1966 finals in England, scoring nine goals and inspiring his unfancied Portugal side to a semi-final against the hosts. In the first group stage, he single-handedly tore apart Brazil, scoring twice to eliminate the 1958 and 1962 champions. Against North Korea, he rescued his team from 3–0 down by scoring four times. He was so popular in England that his waxwork was placed in Madame Tussauds – but it would be the last World Cup Eusebio would appear in, as Portugal failed to qualify for the finals again until 1986.
Tournament 1966 **Games** 6 **Goals** 9

FONTAINE, JUSTE (France, b. 1933) The first of a long line of mercurial French stars, Juste Fontaine combined artistry with clinical finishing in 1958 to claim the record for the most goals scored in a single tournament. His thirteen goals propelled France to the semi-finals, but it was in the third-place playoff against West Germany that Fontaine excelled himself by scoring four times. Tragically, his career was cut short with a broken leg just two years later.
Tournament 1958 **Games** 6 **Goals** 13

GARRINCHA (Brazil, b. 1933 d. 1983) Manoel dos Santos Francisco was born a cripple, and as a child underwent a series of operations that left his left leg permanently twisted. Nevertheless, Garrincha ('Little Bird') became a footballing legend, a World Cup winner in 1958 and 1962 and a rival to Pelé for the title of greatest Brazilian footballer of all time. Defences were bamboozled by his dribbling, goalkeepers by his banana shot. The 1966 defeat against Hungary was not only his last game but the only time he had ever appeared on a losing side for Brazil. Sadly, off the pitch his personal life was a mess of marital and financial problems. He died of alcohol poisoning, impoverished and largely forgotten, in 1983 at the age of 49.
Tournaments 1958, 1962, 1966 **Games** 12 **Goals** 5

HURST, GEOFF (England, b. 1941) Hurst earns his place in the legends list simply because of his exploits on that hot July day in 1966 when he scored the first – and so far only – hat trick in a World Cup final. A late replacement for the injured Jimmy Greaves, Hurst grabbed his opportunity with both hands. He scored the vital goal against Argentina in the quarter-final then let rip in the final against West Germany. His third goal, rifled in from the edge of the penalty area, remains an iconic image of England's greatest tournament.

Tournaments 1966, 1970 **Games** 6 **Goals** 5

JAIRZINHO (Brazil, b. 1944) Another Brazilian graces the list of legends. Jairzinho played in three tournaments between 1966 and 1974, but like so many of his teammates he was at his bewitching best in Mexico 1970. Despite breaking a leg the previous season, he returned on top form and became the only player to score in every match including the final (Ghiggia of Uruguay scored in every round in 1950, but Uruguay only played 4 games.). His seven goals amounted to a masterclass in the finisher's art, ranging from long-range thunderbolts to delicate chip-ins. In fact his only dodgy goal was the 71st-minute mis-kick that put Brazil 3–1 ahead in the final. Although he failed to reproduce his best form in 1974, Jairzinho continued as a mainstay of the Brazil side, eventually winning his 80th and final cap in 1982 when he was 38 years old.

Tournaments 1966, 1970, 1974 **Games** 16 **Goals** 9

KOCSIS, SANDOR (Hungary, b. 1929 d. 1978) Top scorer in the 1954 tournament with eleven goals, Kocsis was a phenomenal header of the ball and earned the soubriquet 'The Man with the Golden Head'. Alongside Puskás he was part of the magical Hungary side that laid waste to all before them prior to the World Cup, scored 24 goals in four matches in the tournament, yet choked spectacularly to lose in the final to Germany. Who knows what Hungary might have achieved had the country not been invaded by the Soviet Union in 1956. By the time the 1958 finals came around, Kocsis was playing in Spain and decided not to risk returning home. He retired in 1966 aged 37 and died in 1978 at the shockingly young age of 49.

Tournament 1954 **Games** 5 **Goals** 11

LATO, GRZEGORZ (Poland, b. 1950) Lato's hair might have visibly thinned over the course of three World Cup tournaments, but his appetite for the game remained throughout. He began in 1974 as a speedy right-winger, but his all-round game impressed almost as much as his goalscoring. That year he even overshadowed the prodigious Gerd Muller to become top scorer with seven. As the years passed and his speed diminished Lato amended his game accordingly and became even more influential. Although the Polish team misfired in 1978, in 1982 Lato and Zbigniew Boniek led the side to their second bronze medal in eight years.

Tournaments 1974, 1978, 1982 **Games** 20 **Goals** 10

MARADONA, DIEGO (Argentina, b. 1960) Diego Armando Maradona's fans call him the greatest player ever, and even his detractors would argue that the only thing that keeps him behind Pelé in the pantheon is his disciplinary record. Quite simply, on his day Maradona was an unstoppable force, a whirlwind talent able to unpick the tightest defences and beat lesser teams virtually single-handed. Left out of the squad in 1978, Maradona erupted onto the world stage four years later, destroying Hungary with two goals, but was let down by an ageing side that lacked the teeth for a fight and were dumped out in the second group stage. In 1986 in Mexico, Maradona was on a stage all of his own. Forget the 'Hand of God', if you can. Think instead of the second goal against England, and the two against Belgium in the semi-final. Think of how Maradona's desire to win forced an average team to victory in the final. In 1990 he led his side to the final once again, but this time the West Germans got their revenge in an uninspiring match. Four years later, Maradona arrived in the USA determined to go out with a bang, but it was a tournament too far for a 34-year-old who had already developed a liking for the high life during his time playing in Spain and Italy. He lasted two games before

being caught with the stimulant ephedrine in his system. His tournament and his World Cup career were over in one fell swoop. It was a sad end, but Maradona had already done enough for the good memories to eclipse the bad.
Tournaments 1982, 1986, 1990, 1994 **Games** 21 **Goals** 8

NEESKENS, JOHANN (Holland, b. 1951) Neeskens was an integral member of the great Dutch side of the 1970s which transformed the way in which football was played, reached the World Cup finals of 1974 and 1978, yet won nothing and is therefore remembered as one of the great underachieving sides. Neeskens scored five goals in the 1974 tournament, including a sensational chip against Brazil and, of course, the penalty that gave Holland a second-minute lead in the final against West Germany. Although he didn't get on the scoresheet in 1978, he was again instrumental in guiding the Dutch to their second successive final.
Tournaments 1974, 1978 **Games** 13 **Goals** 5

OVERATH, WOLFGANG (West Germany, b. 1943) Wolfgang Overath was a mainstay of the West German team for three World Cups and a supremely talented midfielder in his own right. He was a member of the 1966 side that lost to England in the final, but was undoubtedly at his best in 1970 when he was voted best midfielder of the tournament by the international media. He only scored three goals, but contented himself with being a ball-winner and a provider for the predatory West German front men. His international career was capped off in fine style as a member of the World Cup-winning side of 1974, which made him, along with Beckenbauer, one of the select band of players to have won gold, silver and bronze medals in World Cups.
Tournaments 1966, 1970, 1974 **Games** 19 **Goals** 3

PELÉ (Brazil, b. 1940) What can you say? The only man to win three World Cup winners' medals, the youngest-ever winner of a World Cup, scorer of three goals in World Cup finals and twelve in all ... Pelé's list of achievements is part of World Cup folklore. Indeed in many ways Pelé *is* the World Cup. He was just seventeen when selected to play in the 1958 tournament. Many thought he was too young, but they were soon made to eat their words as the teenager stole the show with a goal in the quarter-final, a hat trick in the semi-final and a brace in the final that included one of the greatest goals in World Cup history. In 1962 and 1966 his participation was curtailed through injury and brutish tackling, but in 1970 he returned in magisterial form, guiding a stellar team to World Cup success with a mixture of almost casual brilliance and deadly finishing. As important as how he played was the manner in which he conducted himself on the pitch. Pelé believed passionately in sportsmanship and the pursuit of individual excellence, and was quick to congratulate those who demonstrated those qualities. After beating England 1–0, the first person he sought out to swap shirts with was Bobby Moore, who had played the best game of his illustrious career that sweltering day in León. Although he retired from international football more than 35 years ago, Pelé remains a legend in the game.

Tournaments 1958, 1962, 1966, 1970 **Games** 14 **Goals** 12

RUMMENIGGE, KARL-HEINZ (West Germany, b. 1955) It was always going to be a tough job following the likes of Helmut Rahn, Uwe Seeler and Gerd Muller as the leader of the West German front line, but Karl-Heinz Rummenigge not only scored goals but led the side to two World Cup finals as captain, a worthy successor to Franz Beckenbauer. His first appearance was in 1978, when he acquitted himself well, scoring three goals in a misfiring team. In 1982 he was at the height of his powers, scoring five goals despite a rapidly deteriorating knee. There were those who said he should not have played in the final against Italy, but to many in the young German side Rummenigge was a figurehead. In the end it was Italy who won the Cup, not West Germany who lost it. In 1986, aged 31, Rummenigge was captain again, and again he led his side to the final despite being hampered by injury. His 95th and last international was the final against Argentina in which, typically, he scored a goal.

Tournaments 1978, 1982, 1986 **Games** 19 **Goals** 9

SEELER, UWE (West Germany, b. 1936) Brought into the West German squad shortly after their 1954 tournament win, Uwe Seeler went on to play in four World Cups, scoring in every one, and captain his team in the 1966 final against England. His 21 appearances was a record only bettered in recent years by his fellow countryman Lothar Matthaus and Italy's Paolo Maldini. Short, stocky and powerful, Seeler was the blueprint for West German strikers in the 1960s and 1970s and his nine goals belied the chaos he was capable of creating in opposition penalty areas.
Tournaments 1958, 1962, 1966, 1970 **Games** 21 **Goals** 9

TOMASZEWSKI, JAN (Poland, b. 1948) Dismissed as a clown by Brian Clough, Jan Tomaszewski was anything but. His heroics knocked England out of the 1974 World Cup at the qualifying stage, and his consistent brilliance between the sticks helped unfancied Poland to third place in West Germany. His forte was saving penalties. In 1974 he became the first goalkeeper to save two in the same tournament, denying Tapper of Sweden and Hoeness of West Germany. But his record of five clean sheets in eleven World Cup games stands alongside the very best in World Cup history.
Tournaments 1974, 1978 **Games** 11 **Goals conceded** 8 **Clean sheets** 5

VALDERRAMA, CARLOS (Colombia, b. 1961) Best known for his vast mane of yellow hair, Carlos Valderrama was also an inspirational captain and a midfielder reckoned at his prime to be the very best in South America. Known as 'El Pibe' (the kid), Valderrama was one of few players to have captained his country in three World Cups. Although Colombia as a whole flattered to deceive, it was not for the want of trying on Valderrama's behalf. His biggest World Cup moment was when he dribbled past several players and delivered a pinpoint pass to teammate Freddie Rincon, who scored the necessary equaliser three minutes into injury time against eventual winners West Germany in 1990. That goal meant Colombia qualified for the second round. In 1994 Colombia disappointed again, and were knocked out in the first round, while in France four years later, at the age of 37, Valderrama's efforts were once again in vain.

Tournaments 1990, 1994, 1998 **Games** 10 **Goals** 1

WALTER, FRITZ (West Germany, b. 1920 d. 2002) Although the prime of his career was lost to World War II, at the age of 34 Fritz Walter led West Germany back into the international fold and to unexpected World Cup glory in Switzerland. Thrashed 8–3 by the unstoppable Hungarians in a group match, few gave the Germans a prayer when the two sides met again in the final. Yet despite being two goals down in the first 10 minutes, Walter's never-say-die approach inspired his teammates (including brother Ottmar) to a famous comeback. In 1958, aged 38, he led the team once again in Sweden. This time even his efforts were in vain as the Germans went out in the semi-finals. Walter then retired, but in 1962 national manager Herberger made a concerted effort to persuade the 42-year-old to make one last effort in Chile. Wisely, Walter said no. His place in World Cup legend was already assured (he would also be voted into the German team of the century in 1999).

Tournaments 1954, 1958 **Games** 11 **Goals** 3

YASHIN, LEV (USSR, b. 1929 d. 1990) The great Soviet goalkeeper Lev Yashin was not just a superbly agile shot-stopper, he was an innovator who, in his three World Cup tournaments, changed the face of goalkeeping and brought it into the modern age. Before Yashin, keepers were simply the last line of defence and rarely strayed from their own goal line. Yashin changed all that. He would roam his penalty area like a caged tiger, regarding himself as a fifth outfield defender, a sweeper in effect. He preferred to punch the ball to safety rather than catch it, hoping to start a counter-attack from the speedy Soviet wingers. First-choice goalkeeper for thirteen years, Yashin inspired his team to a World Cup semi-final in 1966 when he was 37 and, to many observers, at his best. Certainly his fitness and longevity paved the way for the likes of Dino Zoff and Peter Shilton, who were still at the top of their games into their forties. Tragically, Yashin did not enjoy the best of health in retirement. In 1986 a knee injury led to the amputation of his leg – and just four years later, at the age of just 61, he died of complications following further surgery.

Tournaments 1958, 1962, 1966 **Games** 13 **Goals conceded** 18 **Clean sheets** 4

ZOFF, DINO (Italy, b. 1942) Another veteran goalkeeper on the roster of World Cup legends, the great Dino Zoff is the oldest player to win the World Cup and the only goalkeeper to captain a cup-winning side. A colossus at the heart of a parsimonious Italian defence, Zoff, at the age of 40, gave the likes of Bruno Conti and Marco Tardelli the confidence to operate as playmakers in the 1982 tournament. With Paolo Rossi poaching up front, Italy cruised to the title. Zoff first came to prominence in Italy's 1968 European Championship-winning team, but was dropped for the 1970 World Cup. He returned in 1974 and kept goal throughout three tournaments, conceding just sixteen goals.

Tournaments 1974, 1978, 1982 **Games** 17 **Goals conceded** 16 **Clean sheets** 5

MONTEVIDEO NASTY

There is a whiff of controversy in every World Cup, some more pungent than others, and the inaugural finals of 1930 were no exception. Indeed the competition in Uruguay was only two days old when all hell broke loose. Having comfortably won their first tie 4–1 against Mexico – the first ever World Cup match – France were drawn against Argentina, and found themselves right in the middle of a bitter South American feud. Problems began before the game, when the Argentine supporters, having arrived in ten boats, were brusquely searched for weapons by the Uruguayan police. With tensions running high, and the Uruguayans supporting the French, there were disturbances inside the ground when France had a man sent off and Argentina took the lead with just nine minutes remaining. But this was nothing compared with the mayhem that ensued three minutes later when the French player Marcel Langiller raced the length of the pitch and seemed certain to score, only for the Brazilian referee to blow for full time. The pitch was invaded, and order was only restored when the referee – under advice from his linesman – realised his error. It was to no avail, however, as Argentina held out to win the game, prompting another pitch invasion and very nearly a diplomatic incident as the Argentine delegation threatened to quit the competition and go home.

BLOOD AND GUTS

One of the bloodiest encounters in World Cup history took place in the 1938 finals in France when Brazil and Czechoslovakia met each other in a first-round clash in Bordeaux. From the outset, both teams set about each other with gusto bordering on violence. Brazil's Procopio was sent off for an unprovoked assault on Nejedly in the first half but, with the South Americans leading 1–0, things really kicked off after the interval. Riha and Machado became embroiled in a punch-up and were dismissed, Nejedly was stretchered off with a broken leg and Czech goalkeeper Planicka suffered a broken arm. When the dust settled, the match ended with nineteen players on the pitch, all but two of them having suffered some sort of injury. The match also finished 1–1, which meant the intriguing prospect of a replay. Fortunately this passed off without incident – mainly due to the fact that Brazil fielded nine new players and Czechoslovakia six. The Brazilians won the replay 2–1.

BRAVE SINDELAR

An added bonus for Germany following the annexation of Austria in 1938 was that they found themselves with the cream of Austria's national football side at their disposal. Indeed five Austrians played in the German team in that year's World Cup finals in France. One who refused to be assimilated was Mathias Sindelar, a stylish forward whose stance made him a national hero. But his defiance was no shallow gesture. Sindelar was devastated by the German invasion of his homeland, and a year later killed himself, unable to live under Hitler's rule.

NO FINAL

Uruguay were crowned World Cup winners in 1950 – although there was no final that year. Instead, FIFA and the host nation Brazil had devised a crackpot scheme in which the winners of four qualifying groups went into a final group. The winners of this group would be crowned champions. Any chance of the system working was dashed before the competition started, when only thirteen teams turned up. This meant that Uruguay were in a group that consisted of just themselves and Bolivia. Having dispatched their lowly South American rivals 8–0, the Uruguayans proceeded to the final group having played two games less than everyone else. Although Brazil gave them a run for their money, a 2–1 victory in the packed Maracana Stadium was enough to give Uruguay their second trophy in twenty years.

GREAT GAMES: Italy 4–3 West Germany, 1970

After a tight 90 minutes had ended 1–1, this all-European semi-final exploded in extra time as the sapping Mexican heat forced errors from two solid defences. Having conceded a killer equaliser in the final minute, Italy went from bad to worse four minutes into extra time when Poletti and goalkeeper Albertosi got confused and allowed the predatory Gerd Muller to sneak in and score. Four minutes later, though, the Italians were back – this time from a German mistake. Held, normally a forward, got into a tangle in his own box following a Riva free kick and Burgnich was on hand to smash the ball home from close range. The rollercoaster continued unabated as Riva put the Italians in front with a smart turn and shot, only for Muller to head the equaliser. Straight from the kickoff Boninsegna skinned the exhausted Schulz on the left and crossed for Rivera to sidefoot the ball calmly into the net. This fifth extra-time goal proved to be the last, and Italy were on their way to the final.

THE BROTHERS CHANOV

Brothers have been part of the same World Cup squad several times. But Victor and Vyacheslav Chanov are unique. They were in the 1982 Soviet Union squad, both as goalkeepers. However, neither of them played a match as the great Rinat Dassajev was first choice.

NO SECOND CHANCE FOR THE CAPTAIN

Captaining a winning side in the World Cup is a once-in-a-lifetime experience. But despite the best efforts of captains throughout history, none has done it twice. Diego Maradona captained Argentina to victory in 1986 and to a silver medal in 1990. Dunga of Brazil won as captain in 1994 and lost the final in 1998. Karl-Heinz Rummenigge is the only captain to lose two World Cup finals (1982 and 1986).

WE'LL BE BACK – AFTER THE WAR

Erik Nilsson of Sweden and Alfred Bickel of Switzerland are the only men to have played in the World Cup both before and after World War II. They both appeared in 1938 and 1950.

GOAL INCENTIVE

Winning the 1990 World Cup was not a realistic option for the United Arab Emirates, and sure enough they were knocked out after three straight defeats in the group stage. However, this was not for the want of trying – and indeed at times it seemed the entire team was intent on scoring a goal. The reason for their enthusiasm was revealed later. It turned out that whoever scored a goal would be rewarded with a Rolls-Royce. Khalid Ismael and Ali Juma'a duly scored the UAE's only goals and drove away from Italy with smiles on their faces.

PASSARELLA PREFERS REAL MEN

As a player and captain of the World Cup-winning Argentina side of 1978, Daniel Passarella provided the steel backbone that allowed the likes of Kempes, Luque and Ardiles to strut their stuff. When he graduated to manager in 1994, he proved that he had lost none of his no-nonsense approach. Long-haired players and players with earrings were told in no uncertain terms that they did not have a future in the Argentine team. There were complaints – but when the players realised Passarella was serious even Gabriel Batistuta got his flowing locks cut so as not to miss the World Cup.

CONTROVERSIAL TO THE LAST

Harald Schumacher, West Germany's goalkeeper and twice World Cup finalist, is perhaps best known for his assault on French defender Patrick Battiston in the 1982 semi-final. After losing his second World Cup final in 1986, he said he wanted to come back in 1990 and win the cup at his third attempt. But in 1987 he wrote a book and claimed 90 per cent of the players in the German Bundesliga did drugs! He was never picked for the German squad again after that. He went to Turkey and played league soccer there instead.

GONE IN 60 SECONDS

José Batista of Uruguay was sent off after just 56 seconds against Scotland in 1986. That is the fastest dismissal in World Cup history. His foul on Gordon Strachan gave French referee Joël Quiniou no choice. Uruguay kept the score at 0–0, however, and progressed to the next round at the expense of Scotland.

PENALTY KINGS

Penalty shoot-outs have played a vital part in recent World Cups. West Germany and Argentina have the best records, winning all three shoot-outs they have participated in. Italy on the other hand, have taken part in four and won just one — against France in the 2006 World Cup final.

FLAG OF CONVENIENCE

Five players who each have appeared for two nations in World Cups: José Altafini (then known as Mazzola) for Brazil in 1958 and Italy in 1962; Luis Monti for Argentina in 1930 and Italy in 1934; Ferenc Puskás for Hungary in 1954 and Spain 1962; José Santamaria for Uruguay in 1954 and Spain in 1962; and Robert Prosinecki for Yugoslavia in 1990 and Croatia in 1998. The rules have now changed, and no player can play for more than one country.

UNBEATEN ZENGA

Italian goalkeeper Walter Zenga holds the record of longest unbeaten run in World Cup history. He played 517 minutes (almost six games) without letting in a goal in the 1990 tournament. Claudio Caniggia of Argentina ended his run in the semi-final, which Italy eventually lost on penalties.

X FINALLY RATED

When Daniel Xuereb of France came on as a substitute for Bruno Bellone in the semi-final against West Germany in 1986, it was a red-letter day for statistics nuts. The X meant that every letter in the alphabet had been used in players' surnames since the start of the championships in 1930.

GET THAT GOALKEEPER OFF!

Muampa Kazadi was the first goalkeeper to be replaced for any other reason than injury in World Cup history, when Zaïre were 0–3 down versus Yugoslavia after just 22 minutes in 1974. The only other time a goalkeeper has been replaced for any other reason than injury was in the third-place playoff in

USA 1994, when Bulgarian keeper Mihailov was substituted at half time with Sweden leading 4—0. Nikolov came in for him and kept a clean sheet in the second half.

CRUYFF'S TURN

The 1974 World Cup match between Sweden and Holland ended in a stale 0—0 draw, but was enlivened by a moment of magic by Dutch skipper Johan Cruyff, who bamboozled a Swedish defender with a drag-back manoeuvre which became known simply as the 'Cruyff Turn':

1. Cruyff, on the left wing, shapes to cross the ball.

2. He stops abruptly and lifts his leg at a 45-degree angle.

3. He drags the ball back behind his standing leg with the inside of his foot.

4. Now he spins round so his shoulders and hips are in line with the ball.

5. Defender beaten, Cruyff continues on his way.

GOAL-CRAZY FRANCE

In 1958, the French team won the third-place playoff 6–3 against West Germany – and in doing so took their goal tally for the tournament to an extraordinary 23 in just six games. Supreme marksman was Juste Fontaine, who bagged thirteen goals, including four in the last match. It was a remarkable turn-around for the French who the previous November had been crushed 4–0 by England.

FERRINI FAILS TO WALK

Sent off by English referee Ken Aston just four minutes into his team's match with hosts Chile in 1962, Italian inside-forward Giorgio Ferrini refused to leave the pitch. Eventually, ten minutes later, the Italian was escorted to the changing rooms by two hefty armed policemen. It was not long before he was joined for an early bath by teammate Mario David as the match known as the Battle of Santiago lurched into violent anarchy. With just nine of their men remaining on the pitch, Italy managed to hang on for 73 minutes before Chile opened the scoring, going on to win the match 2–0.

A TROPHY FIT FOR CHAMPIONS

The Jules Rimet Trophy was the original prize for winning the World Cup. Originally called simply the World Cup or Coupe du Monde, it was renamed in 1946 to honour the FIFA President Jules Rimet who in 1929 passed a vote to initiate the competition. It was designed by Abel Lafleur, standing 35cm (14in) high and weighing 3.8kg (8½lb) and made of gold-plated sterling silver. It was in the shape of a cup, incorporating a statuette of Nike, the ancient Greek goddess of victory.

ANIMALS?

England manager Alf Ramsey was so infuriated by what he perceived as foul play by Argentina in England's quarter-final match in the 1966 World Cup, he not only forbade his side to swap jerseys with the South Americans, but labelled them 'animals'. But were they? Argentina were indeed reduced to ten men after their captain Rattin was sent off – but his offence was more dissent than foul play. And in a letter to the *Times* a few days later, Lord Lovat of the Guards Club pointed out that in fact Argentina had only committed 19 fouls in the game, compared with 33 by England.

1970 INNOVATIONS

The 1970 World Cup in Mexico saw two innovations that have become standard practice in football matches ever since. First, substitutes were allowed for the first time. Second, yellow and red cards were introduced.

FOOTBALL IS NOT A GAME OF LIFE AND DEATH – OR IS IT?

In order to qualify for the 1970 finals in Brazil, Honduras and El Salvador were drawn together in the same group. The rivalry between the two sides was such that the result was very nearly all-out war. The mayhem erupted as follows:

Prior to their match in Honduras, the El Salvador team were kept awake all night in their hotel by gangs of home supporters. Honduras won the match 1–0 through a last-minute goal. Back in El Salvador, eighteen-year-old Amelia Bolianos was so distraught, she seized her father's pistol and shot herself through the heart. Her funeral was shown live on TV, ensuring that the second meeting between the two sides was conducted in an atmosphere of mounting hysteria.

On the eve of the second leg, El Salvador fans broke into the Honduras hotel and pelted the players with rotten eggs and dead rats. The home team won 3–0 and Honduras required an armed convoy to get them back to the airport. Two of their fans were killed after the game, and many others kicked and beaten as they attempted to flee back across the border.

Incredibly, the group finished with both El Salvador and Honduras forced
to play a sudden-death playoff. Four days beforehand, diplomatic relations
between the two nations were severed – but this was nothing compared
with the three days of fighting that ensued after El Salvador had succeeded in
winning the tie 3–2 in extra time. When it was over, more than 3,000 people
were dead.

WORLD CUP RECORDS

- **Oldest player** Cameroon's Roger Milla, who was 42 years and 39 days old
when he played against Russia in 1994.

- **Youngest player** Norman Whiteside of Northern Ireland, who was just 17
years and 41 days old when he played against Yugoslavia in 1982.

- **Shortest World Cup career in terms of minutes on the field** Tunisia's Khemais
Labidi, who played two minutes against Mexico in 1978, and Argentina's
Marcelo Trobbiani, who played the last two minutes of his country's 3–2
final win over West Germany in 1986.

- **First World Cup substitute** Anatoli Puzach of the Soviet Union against Mexico
in 1970. He replaced Shesterniev. Substitutes were never used until the
1970 World Cup.

- **First goalkeeper to be substituted** Steve Adamache of Romania against Brazil.
He was injured and replaced by Necula Raducanu in 1970.

- **Fastest substitution** 1998, when Italy's Alessandro Nesta was replaced by
Giuseppe Bergomi in the match against Austria after only four minutes.

- **The man who has refereed most matches** 8 – Joël Quiniou (France, 1986–
1994), Benito Archundia (Mexico, 2006–2010) and Jorge Larrionda

(Uruguay, 2006–2010). He was in charge of eight matches between 1986 and 1994 with four of them coming in USA '94. Nicolaj Latychev (Russia, 1962), José Ramiz Wright (Brazil, 1990) and Jan Langenus (Belgium, 1930) have also refereed four times in one tournament – which is a record also.

⊛ **Youngest referee** Juan Gardeazábal of Spain, aged 24 years and 193 days when he took charge of France vs Paraguay in the 1958 finals.

⊛ **Oldest referee** George Reader of England, aged 53 years and 236 days when he reffed the Brazil–Uruguay World Cup-deciding match in 1950.

⊛ **Youngest coach** Juan José Tramutola of Argentina, aged 27 years and 267 days when his country opened its campaign against France in 1930.

⊛ **Oldest coach** Otto Rehhagel of Greece, 71 days and 317 days in the 2010 finals.

EDUCATION COMES FIRST

In the 1930 group stage, Argentina faced South American rivals Mexico without their captain, Ferreyra, after he decided to return home to sit his university exams. It didn't make much difference – his side were 6–3 winners, with centre-forward Stabile the first man to bag a World Cup hat trick.

NO CROWD TROUBLE

When Romania met Peru in a group stage match in the 1930 finals, a crowd of just 300 people turned out to watch. Unfortunately, the match was played on Bastille Day, a public holiday in Uruguay, and most people in Montevideo had better things to do with their time than watch two foreign teams play football. By contrast, when Uruguay played in the same stadium just four days later, nearly 100,000 fans filled the terraces.

NO COACH

Uruguay, hosts and winners of the 1930 World Cup finals, played all their matches without a coach. The players decided on the line-ups and the tactics between themselves over a convivial supper the night before a match.

SHOT PUTTERS

In 1930, the USA team was nicknamed 'The Shot Putters' by the French squad because of their muscular builds. The side was mostly made up of expat Brits who had conveniently been granted Green Card work permits by the US government in time for the finals in Uruguay.

OUT FOR THE COUNT

As touchline protests go, one of most futile was staged by the trainer of the USA side during their group match against Argentina in 1930. Incensed at a refereeing decision, he threw down his medical box in a fit of pique. Unfortunately this succeeded only in smashing a bottle of chloroform, which knocked him out and resulted in him being carried from the pitch. Out for the count, he missed his side being trounced 6–1.

BALLS!

The rivalry between Uruguay and Argentina was such that in the 1930 final, each half was played with a different ball manufactured in each country. Uruguay's 4–2 victory prompted riots in Buenos Aires, during which the Uruguayan embassy was stoned and diplomatic relations were suspended.

BROTHERS IN ARMS

The Evaristo brothers of Argentina were the first to play together in a World Cup final when they turned out against Uruguay in 1930.

URUGUAY ABSENT

Still miffed at the general European apathy that meant only France, Yugoslavia, Romania and Belgium bothered to enter the 1930 finals, Uruguay refused to enter the 1934 competition held in Italy. They remain the only reigning World Cup champions who have failed to defend their title.

ESCAPE ROUTE

Belgian referee John Langenus was so concerned about the repercussions of officiating the 1930 final between Uruguay and Argentina, he not only demanded police protection in the stadium but a guaranteed escape route to the ship on which he and the rest of the Belgian party were staying.

VISIT OF THE DUCE

Italian dictator Benito Mussolini was in no doubt that his presence would inspire his country in their opening game of the 1934 World Cup in Rome. Indeed, a newspaper editorial on the morning of the match crowed that Il Duce would be 'bestowing the privilege of his presence, which would galvanise the two teams more than any other coefficient'. It certainly galvanised the Italians, who crushed the USA 7–1.

POLE APART

Five years before Germany invaded Poland, their 1934 World Cup football team was captained by Fritz Szepan – a Pole.

FATHERS AND SONS

When Patrice Rio appeared for France in the 1978 World Cup finals he was following in the footsteps of his father, Roger, who played for France in the 1934 tournament. Similarly José Vantrola, who played for Mexico in 1970,

was the son of Martin Vantrola, who starred in the Spanish midfield in 1934.
Miguel Alonso played for Spain in Argentina in 1978 and when they hosted the
1982 World Cup finals. His son Xabi was in the Spanish squad which competed
in the 2002 World Cup finals in Japan/South Korea.

HERE COME CUBA

Cuba played Mexico three times during qualifying for the 1938 World Cup and
lost every time. Yet they still made it to the finals in France – as a replacement
for Mexico, who dropped out at the last minute.

DUTCH COURAGE

As World Cup outsiders go, the Dutch East Indies side that made it to the
1938 finals was possibly the most mismatched. Lining up for their first and
last World Cup fixture against the mighty Hungarians, nine of their side were
earning their first caps and eight of them were students. Their captain, Achmad
Nawir, was a doctor whose short-sightedness meant he had to wear spectacles
on the pitch. Unsurprisingly, they were hammered 6–0.

ALL CHANGE FOR ITALY

When Italy played France at the Colombes Stadium in Paris in 1938, a good
proportion of the 58,000 crowd consisted of anti-Fascist Italians who had fled
their homeland in order to escape the regime of dictator Benito Mussolini.
Yet the hail of abuse which greeted their every touch seemed to inspire
the Italians, who weathered tremendous French pressure to finish the first
half level at 1–1. Realising that his side clearly played better in the face of
adversity, Italian manager Vittorio Pozzo sent his team out for the second half
wearing an all-black strip – the preferred colour of the Fascist movement. His
unconventional ploy worked like a charm as, despite the fury of the crowd,
Italy ran out 3–1 winners.

GOALLESS RECORD

The 1958 clash between England and Brazil was the 105th World Cup match and, remarkably, the very first to end goalless.

FIREWORKS

The Maracana stadium in Rio was built especially for the 1950 World Cup – although it was far from being finished in time for the opening match between hosts Brazil and Mexico. Indeed much of the concrete was still drying when a pre-match 21-gun salute erupted on the pitch. Watching from the stands, English referee Arthur Ellis recalled how 'we were peppered with a shower of concrete, fortunately none of it in huge blocks!'

CAN I HAVE A WORD?

No sooner had Brazilian striker Ademir given his side the lead in their first match of the 1950 World Cup against Mexico than he was swamped by fifteen radio commentators and more than twenty newspaper reporters who had run onto the pitch in search of a quote.

LATE KICKOFF

The 1950 tie between Yugoslavia and Switzerland in Belo Horizonte, Brazil, kicked off twenty minutes late while corner flags were found and a line of chairs, reserved for dignitaries, was moved from right next to one of the touchlines. Consequently, the match became the first to be completed under floodlights. The Yugoslavs won 3–0, with two of the goals being scored in the gloom of the last ten minutes.

WISE BEFORE THE EVENT

Prior to their match against Switzerland in 1950, Brazilian coach Flavio Costa arrogantly dismissed his European opponents as 'contenders without importance'. Fittingly, Costa required a police escort from the stadium to protect him from irate Brazil fans after his side could only manage a 2–2 draw.

SOLE REPORTER

The USA's 1–0 win over England in 1950 sent shockwaves around the footballing world – except in the States. Indeed there was only one American reporter in the ground to see the historic victory: Dent McSkimming of the St Louis Post Despatch, who was only present because he happened to be on holiday in Brazil at the time.

YOU'VE GOT TO START SOMEWHERE

The very first World Cup qualifier was played on 11 June 1933. Sweden beat Estonia 6–2.

LONG HAUL FOR THE 'REGGAE BOYZ'

If anyone deserved a place in the 1998 World Cup it was the self-styled 'Reggae Boyz' of Jamaica. After all, in order to reach France they had been forced to play an extraordinary twenty qualifying matches. After all that, they found themselves drawn in a group that included Argentina and Croatia, who thrashed them 5–0 and 3–1 respectively. However, in their last group match against Japan the Reggae Boyz turned on the style and recorded a fine 2–1 win thanks to two goals from Theodore Whitmore. And as far as they were concerned, the result made the long haul worthwhile. 'Did the road really have to end that quick?' said captain Leroy Simpson after the match. 'I'm really ecstatic at the moment. I'm over the moon that we can actually leave the tournament on a high.'

LOWEST ATTENDANCE

It wasn't quite one man and his dog, but when Turkmenistan played Chinese Taipei in a qualifying game at Amman on 7 May 2001, the crowd was just twenty people. Those who could be bothered to attend saw Turkmenistan win by a single goal to nil.

AMATEUR EXCEPT FOR ALFREDO

In 1930 Argentina reached the World Cup final. But due to a row between various factions of the Argentine FA in the intervening four years, the 1934 squad was made up almost entirely of amateur players. Only skipper Alfredo Devincenzi had been capped before.

'STURMTANK'

Robust Hungarian striker Geza Toldi was nicknamed 'Sturmtank' (Storm Tank) because of his frightening physique. In his first game of the 1934 World Cup finals he scored a goal by simply barging the Egyptian goalkeeper into the back of the net – a tactic which was regarded as perfectly acceptable at the time.

ARGENTINA ABSENT

Following their success in reaching the 1930 final, several of Argentina's top players were promptly poached by leading Italian clubs to the extent that one of them, Monti, actually qualified for residence and appeared for the Azzurri in the 1934 finals in Italy. To prevent further defections, the Argentine football authorities banned their star players from travelling to Italy – with the inevitable result that they were knocked out by Sweden in the first round.

ANNEXE

On 12 March 1938, Adolf Hitler invaded Austria. Not surprisingly, the Austrian team was withdrawn from that year's World Cup finals in France. However, five of their leading players (Hahnemann, Raftl, Schmaus, Skoumal, Neumer and Stroh) did play – for Germany, who claimed that since Austria had been annexed, the men qualified for the Fatherland. To Hitler's fury, such rule-bending was to no avail. Germany were eliminated in the first round by Switzerland.

BRAZILIAN ARROGANCE

In 1938 Brazil clearly believed their name was on the Jules Rimet trophy. Having drawn with Czechoslovakia in a bloody first-round match, the South Americans dispatched most of their squad to Marseille in advance of the replay, anticipating a semi-final tie against Italy. The gamble paid off, and they won 2–1. In the semi-final, the Brazilians were so confident of victory that they rested their star strikers Leonidas and Tim and fielded what amounted to a second-string side. This time, the Italians ran out 2–1 winners and proceeded to win their second successive World Cup, leaving Brazil with egg on their faces.

POZZO'S PRETEXT

Vittorio Pozzo is the only man to manage two World Cup-winning sides, leading Italy to the trophy in 1934 and 1938. A keen student of the game, who compiled lengthy dossiers on his opponents, Pozzo was also a keen rule-bender who selected Argentine-born players on the flimsy pretext that they were eligible for Italian national service. 'If they can die for Italy, they can play for Italy!' was one of his maxims.

INDIA BAREFOOT

India withdrew from the 1950 World Cup finals in Brazil after FIFA officials told them they could not play barefoot.

SCOTLAND FEEL THE HEAT

Perhaps believing that Switzerland was snowbound all year round, the Scotland team arrived at the 1954 World Cup finals with kit that included thick woolly jerseys with long sleeves. Unfortunately, temperatures in Basle topped 100°F during their group matches. 'You'd have thought we were going on an expedition to the Antarctic,' said wing-half Tommy Docherty. It was no surprise, therefore, that the Scots were soon on their way home after losing 1–0 to Austria and being crushed 7–0 by Uruguay.

SWISS CAPTAIN

Captain of the 1954 Swiss team was Roger Bocquet, a normally highly competent defender. But, having swept to a 3–0 lead in a group match against Austria, the Swiss inexplicably collapsed to lose 5–4. Prime culprit was Bocquet himself, who gifted a couple of goals and to many observers appeared to be playing as if in a trance. It was only later that it was revealed Bocquet was suffering from a brain tumour and had played against medical advice.

SNOW ON MEXICO

Despite the advantage of playing against European opposition in South America, Mexico were thrashed by France 4–1 in the first ever World Cup match in Montevideo, Uruguay in 1930. Oddly, the Mexicans complained about the weather — as the night before it had snowed.

YOUNG STARTER

Juan José Tramutola was, at 27 years and 267 days, the youngest-ever World Cup coach when he masterminded Argentina's assault on the 1930 tournament in Uruguay.

WHO'S THE BOLIVIAN IN THE BLACK?

Such was the convivial nature of the first World Cup in 1930, when Argentina played Mexico the referee was also the manager of Bolivia, while the linesman was the Romanian boss.

VIVA BOLIVIA

Determined to make a good impression, Bolivia took to the pitch for their 1930 clash against Yugoslavia with each player sporting a letter of the alphabet on the front of his white shirt, forming the words 'Viva Uruguay'. Yugoslavia thrashed them 4—0.

BERET SPORTING ATTIRE

When Bolivia played Brazil in 1930, three players from each side were sporting berets.

MY BROTHER THE PRESIDENT

Star of the 1930 Uruguay side, Pedro Gestido had another claim to fame. His brother Oscar was the country's president.

AMERICAN CLUBS

In order to make up a squad for the 1930 World Cup, selectors from the USA were forced to scour obscure expat clubs for players. Hence while other teams boasted players from the likes of Santos, River Plate and Milan, the Americans came from the likes of Wiebolt Wonderbolts, Detroit Holley Carburettor, Curry Silver Tops and Providence Clamdiggers.

THE BATTLE OF BERNE

It took only three minutes for the 1954 match between Hungary and Brazil
to disintegrate into what one commentator has described as 'psychopathic
violence, disorder and anarchy'. That was how long it took Hungary's
Hidegkuti to score the opening goal, prompting outrageous scenes in which
he was mobbed by the Brazilians and had his shorts ripped off. The rest of the
game was punctuated by a series of increasingly horrific fouls and outrageous
play-acting. English referee Arthur Ellis did his best to control the mayhem,
but meltdown occurred with fifteen minutes remaining and Hungary leading
3–2. Brazil's Santos and Hungary's Bozsik (an upstanding member of the
Hungarian parliament) were sent off for fighting. The Brazilian trainer ran on
to protest and was escorted off the pitch by Swiss police. A few minutes later,
with Hungary now 4–2 ahead, Brazil's Humberto launched a flying kick at
Lorant and was ordered off by Mr Ellis. His departure was delayed by a bizarre
interlude in which the player sank to his knees and begged the referee to be
allowed to stay on the pitch. But if the game itself was a disgrace, worse was to
follow after the final whistle. As the Hungarians celebrated their victory in the
changing room, bottles were thrown at them. Seconds later the lightbulb was
smashed and suddenly the Hungarians found themselves being set upon by the
Brazilians. In the all-out scrap that followed, Hoth was knocked unconscious
and Sebes had his cheek cut open. Had they not already been on their way
home, the Brazilians would surely have been kicked out of the tournament
they had so comprehensively tarnished.

FIRST DEFEAT

Uruguay's 4–2 defeat to Hungary in the semi-final of the 1954 tournament
was their first ever World Cup loss.

PICKLES RIP

In 1966 Pickles the dog found the Jules Rimet trophy and saved the English FA from extreme embarrassment. Unfortunately there wasn't such a happy ending for Pickles himself. In 1971, while chasing a cat up a tree, the dog fell from the lower branches and was hanged by his own lead.

GREAT GAMES: Italy 3–2 Brazil, 1982

Paolo Rossi had been brought in from his match-fixing exile to provide Italy with goals – but up until this second-round match in Barcelona he had barely touched the ball. What a time he picked to wake up, against a Brazil side which had destroyed all before them with a breathtaking display of skill and goalscoring, and which only required a draw to proceed to the semi-finals. Rossi struck after just five minutes with a typical poacher's finish from close range. Brazil hit back almost immediately through the elegant Socrates, but then Cerezo gifted Rossi a second with a stray back-pass. With 68 minutes gone, Falcao blasted home a characteristically sublime long-range shot which surely meant the Brazilians were through. But this was Rossi's day: with sixteen minutes remaining, the little striker turned in the penalty area to shoot past Waldir Perez. Even then there was still time for high drama as Oscar looked certain to score with a header only for veteran Dino Zoff to pull off one of the saves of his career and send Italy into the semis.

REST HOME

West Germany's 3–2 victory over the mighty Hungary side of Hidegkuti, Kocsis and Puskás in the final of the 1954 World Cup was one of the greatest upsets in the history of the competition. But it was also wreathed in controversy. Just days after the final, several of the Germans checked into rest homes. Although they claimed it was to recover from the rigours of the tournament, it was rumoured that the real reason was to recover from the performance-enhancing drugs which had helped them to their first World Cup triumph.

WALES TAKE THE LONG ROAD

Wales have only qualified for the World Cup once, in 1958. Amazingly, their route to the finals in Sweden was courtesy of the Asia/Africa qualifying section. Egypt and Sudan were excluded due to the inflamed Middle East situation, while Indonesia's ongoing political struggles meant they had more pressing matters than qualifying for the World Cup. The fourth member of the group, Israel, was left with no opponent – but tournament regulations insisted that no team other than the host and the holder could proceed to the finals without first playing a qualifying match. As a result, the runners-up in eight other groups drew lots for a place in a special playoff. Wales were the lucky team and, by defeating Israel twice, proceeded to the finals.

HOME COUNTRIES

The 1958 finals in Sweden are the only occasion at which all four Home Union countries have qualified for the latter stages.

THE MIGHTY IRISH

Northern Ireland rarely grace World Cup finals, but when they do they always succeed in defying all expectations. In 1958 the men in green had already signalled their intent by beating Italy 2–1 in Belfast to reach the finals, and once in Sweden the team continued to confound the nay-sayers by pulling off a string of sensational results. In their first game they beat Czechoslovakia 1–0. The next match saw them play the powerful West Germany, holders of the cup. Widely expected to be thrashed, an Irish side including Danny Blanchflower, Derek Dougan and Peter McParland gave the Germans the fright of their lives. Only a Uwe Seeler thunderbolt in the dying minutes secured a 2–2 draw. A comprehensive defeat by Argentina in their next match left the Irish needing to win a playoff against Czechoslovakia. Miraculously, with just nine fit players on the field, Blanchflower's men managed to win in extra time. Despite losing the quarter-final 4–0 to France, the Northern Ireland players returned home as heroes.

DISASTER FOR SCOTLAND!

 In qualifying for World Cup finals, Scotland invariably show a passion and unity of purpose which, for some inexplicable reason, seems to disintegrate the minute their plane lands. Here is their World Cup tale of woe so far: it is not for the fainthearted.

1950

The Scots qualify for Brazil by finishing runners-up to England in a qualifying group based on the Home International championship. However, the Scottish FA petulantly carry out their threat to withdraw from the tournament if they are not British champions.

1954

Having reached Switzerland in fine style, the Scots swiftly self-destruct. They lose to Austria then, after a row with the Scottish FA, manager Andy Beattie quits on the eve of the pool game against Uruguay. The team are duly hammered 7–0, having been sent onto the park in 100-degree heat with woollen, long-sleeved shirts.

1958

The Scottish FA appoint Matt Busby as manager for the tournament in Brazil. Just weeks later, Busby is seriously injured in the Munich air crash and is replaced by Dawson Walker. Despite gaining their first World Cup goal and point in a 1–1 draw with Yugoslavia, the Scots lose three influential players to injury and lose 3–2 to Paraguay. A draw against France would give them a chance of reaching the quarter-finals, but with minutes to go and trailing 2–1, the Scots miss a penalty.

1974

Having missed out on three World Cup finals, the Scots are understandably overjoyed to qualify for West Germany as Britain's sole representatives. So much so that leading players Billy Bremner and Willie Johnston are threatened with expulsion by the Scottish FA after missing a curfew during a warm-up tour in Norway. For a while, things go well on the pitch. A 2–0 win over lowly Zaire is followed by an encouraging goalless draw against the world champions Brazil. A draw will suffice against Yugoslavia, as long as Brazil score less than three clear goals against Zaire. Scotland play abysmally and can only salvage a draw through a last minute goal by Joe Jordan. Inevitably, Brazil win 3–0. Despite remaining the only unbeaten team in the entire tournament, Scotland are on their way home.

1978

The Tartan Army, Britain's sole representatives once again, fly into Argentina on a wave of frenzied expectation, chiefly orchestrated by their manager Ally MacLeod and by the bookies who have laid odds of 8–1 that they will win the competition. There is therefore a huge sense of anticlimax in watching the team utterly humiliated by Peru, who beat them 3–1, and Iran, who contrive a 1–1 draw. Needing to beat Holland by three clear goals to qualify for the next stage, the Scots pull out their best performance of the tournament – but win 3–2. Once again they are on the early flight home, although they are beaten to it by winger Willie Johnston who has already been sent home in disgrace after failing a drugs test.

1982

Leading 3–0 in their first group match against lowly New Zealand, things at last appear to be going to plan for Scotland. But then New Zealand score twice and suddenly it is panic stations. Although two late Scottish goals calm the nerves slightly, it does not bode well for the Tartan Army – especially as their next opponents are Brazil. And so it proves. Despite scoring one of the goals of the tournament through David Narey, the Scots are skewered by the skills of Zico, Falcao, Socrates and Junior, and are fortunate to escape with a 4–1 hiding. Needing to beat the USSR to progress, there is a sad inevitability about the gallant but futile 2–2 draw which eliminates them on goal difference.

WORLD CUP FACTS

MOST PARTICIPATIONS (TEAM)

Brazil............................20
Germany 18
Italy 18
Argentina 16
Mexico 15

MOST APPEARANCES BY A PLAYER

Lothar Matthaus (West Germany/Germany) 25, 1982–98
Paolo Maldini (Italy) 23, 1990–2002
Uwe Seeler (West Germany) 21, 1958–1970
Wladislaw Zmuda (Poland) 21, 1970–1986
Diego Maradona (Argentina) 21, 1982–1994

MOST GOALS IN ONE COMPETITION

Hungary 27, 1954
West Germany 25, 1954
France 23, 1958
Brazil 22, 1950
Brazil 19, 1970

MOST COMPETITIONS BY A PLAYER

Antonio Carbajal (Mexico) 5, 1950–66
Lothar Matthaus
(West Germany/Germany) 5, 1982–98

MOST HAT TRICKS

2, Sándor Kocsis (Hungary, 1954), Just Fontaine (France, 1958), Gerd Müller (West Germany, 1970), and Gabriel Batistuta (Argentina, 1994 and 1998).

YOUNGEST GOALSCORER
17 years and 239 days, Pelé
(Brazil, vs Wales, 1958).

OLDEST GOALSCORER
42 years and 39 days, Roger Milla
(Cameroon, vs Russia, 1994).

BIGGEST WINS
Hungary 10–1 El Salvador, 1982
Hungary 9–0 South Korea, 1954
Yugoslavia 9–0 Zaire, 1974
Sweden 8–0 Cuba, 1938
Uruguay 8–0 Bolivia, 1950
Germany 8–0 Saudi Arabia, 2002

WORLD CUP STOLEN

It was perhaps the proudest moment in the history of the English Football
Association – but it was to turn into a huge embarrassment.

Having been chosen to host the 1966 World Cup finals, the FA were
obviously keen to promote the event at every opportunity. In March that
year, the committee got hold of the £30,000 solid gold Jules Rimet trophy
and put it on display at the 'Sport with Stamps' exhibition at Central Hall in
Westminster, London.

During a church service taking place in another part of the building, the
unthinkable happened and, despite the presence of two guards, the trophy
was stolen. In what was thought to be an opportunistic theft, the thieves left
stamps worth £3 million.

According to police, a 'suspicious-looking man' was seen in the building
at the time of the theft. He was described as being in his early thirties, of

average height with thin lips, greased black hair and a possible scar on his face. Vice-chairman of the Football Association Council Jack Stewart was reluctant to accept blame for the trophy's disappearance. But he admitted: 'We are responsible for it in the end because we are the organizing association.'

This was little comfort to Brazil, who had been holders of the Cup for the previous eight years, after winning both the 1958 and 1962 competitions.

After several days, it seemed that the famous trophy was gone for ever. Then, on 27 March, a week after the theft, David Corbett, a Thames lighterman, saw his mongrel dog Pickles scratching at something wrapped in newspaper in a garden near his South London home. To his astonishment, inside was the Jules Rimet trophy. A little over two months later, Corbett was watching as the trophy was lifted by victorious England skipper Bobby Moore.

THE MATTHEWS FINALS

England's Stanley Matthews was not only the oldest player at the 1950 World Cup finals, aged 35, but also at the 1954 finals in Switzerland, where he appeared aged 39.

SWEDEN'S CRAZY RULE

Sweden pulled off one of the shocks of the 1950 World Cup when they defeated Italy 3–2 in a group match in Sao Paulo. More remarkably, they did so without three of their best players. The inside-forward trio of Gren, Nordahl and Liedholm had been signed by AC Milan the previous season, and the Swedish FA refused to pick players who played for foreign clubs. This policy was quickly changed after the World Cup, when almost the entire Swedish squad were signed by Italian clubs.

THE FINALS

1930

URUGUAY (1) 4 Dorado 12, Cea 57, Iriarte 68, Castro 89
ARGENTINA (2) 2 Peucelle 20, Stabile 37
Date 30 July 1930   **Venue** Centenario, Montevideo
Attendance 93,000   **Referee** John Langenus (BEL)

Uruguay took the lead through Dorado, but the goal was cancelled out eight minutes later when winger Peucelle dodged two tackles to fire home from the edge of the box. Argentina, playing with flair and skill compared with the hosts' rugged style, then stunned the home crowd by taking the lead through Stabile. In the second half, however, Uruguay's physical approach and the effect of the huge partisan crowd began to tell. Cea levelled the scores after 57 minutes and then Argentina wilted under waves of Uruguayan pressure. First Iriarte beat the keeper with a dipping long-range shot, then, in the dying seconds Castro looped a header into the net to confirm the win.

URUGUAY Ballestro, Nasazzi (c), Mascheroni, Andrade, Fernandez, Gestido, Dorado, Scarone, Castro, Cea, Iriarte

ARGENTINA Botasso, Della Torre, Paternoster, J Evaristo, Monti, Suarez, Peucelle, Varallo, Stabile, Ferreira (c), M Evaristo

---

1934

ITALY (0) (1) 2 Orsi 81, Schiavo 95
CZECHOSLOVAKIA (0) (1) 1 (AET) Puc 71
Date 10 June 1934   **Venue** Nazionale del PNF, Rome
Attendance 50,000   **Referee** Ivan Eklind (SWE)

A grim battle of attrition saw Italy and Czechoslovakia grind out a goalless first half. The second looked to be heading the same way until a moment of genius from Czech winger Puc transformed the match at 71 minutes. Receiving the ball way out, he sliced through the Italian defence and drew the keeper before smashing it home inside the near post. It was a remarkable goal because only minutes earlier Puc had been carried off dazed from a crunching tackle and had to be given a whiff of ammonia to unscramble his senses. Suddenly the Czechs were rampant, hitting the post and firing just over the bar. Then, with nine minutes remaining and totally against the run of play, Italy equalised. Orsi collected the ball on the edge of the box, dummied to shoot with his left foot then curled an unstoppable shot into the net with the outside of his right. The crowd – which included Mussolini – went wild; the game went into extra time. Five minutes in, Guaita found Schiavo unmarked on the edge of the box and his low cross shot beat the Czech keeper and flew into the net. There was no way back for Czechoslovakia and Italy had secured their first World Cup.

ITALY Combi (c), Monzeglio, Allemandi, Ferraris, Monti, Bertolini, Guaita, Meazza, Schiavo, Ferrari, Orsi

CZECHOSLOVAKIA Planicka (c), Zenisek, Ctyroky, Kostalek, Cambal, Krcil, Junek, Svoboda, Sobotka, Nejedly, Puc

1938

ITALY (3) 4 Colaussi 6, 35, Piola 16, 82
HUNGARY (1) 2 Titkos 7, Sarosi 69
Date 19 June 1938   **Venue** Stade Colombes, Paris
Attendance 45,124   **Referee** Georges Capdeville (FRA)

A second successive World Cup for Italy, but achieved with considerably more ease than their first. The Italians were ahead after just six minutes, but despite equalising almost immediately the Hungarian defence spent the first half at sixes and sevens as Piola and Biavati cut them to ribbons. Piola restored the lead after 16 minutes, having just hit the post, then was instrumental in creating Colaussi's second after 35 minutes. Shell-shocked, Hungary rallied in the second half and pulled a goal back through Sarosi — but with eight minutes remaining Piola sent Briavati away down the right-hand side and was on hand to hammer home the cross. Italian skipper Meazza received the trophy with a Fascist salute to the watching Mussolini, a last symbolic act as Europe teetered on the brink of war.

ITALY Olivieri, Foni, Rava, Serantoni, Andreolo, Locatelli, Biavati, Meazza (c), Piola, Ferrari, Colaussi

HUNGARY Szabo, Polgar, Biro, Szalay, Szucs, Lazar, Sas, Vincze, Sarosi (c), Zsengeller, Titkos

---

1950

URUGUAY (0) 2 Schiaffino 66, Ghiggia 79
BRAZIL (0) 1 Friaca 47
Date 16 July 1950   **Venue** Maracana, Rio de Janeiro
Attendance 205,000 **Referee** George Reader (ENG)

FIFA, in their wisdom, decided that the first World Cup after the war would not be decided by a final tie but by a final group, the winners of which would be crowned champions. So it was that on 9 July Brazil, Spain, Sweden and Uruguay began a tortuous series of round-robin matches that would finally climax nine days later. When Brazil demolished Sweden and Spain 7–1 and 6–1 respectively, they must have felt they had one hand on the trophy. In their final pool match they needed only a draw against Uruguay — who had drawn against Spain and scored a last-gasp winner against Sweden — to confirm their position as undisputed champions. Yet, in front of a staggering 205,000 people in the Maracana Stadium — the biggest crowd ever to watch a football match — Brazil fluffed their lines. Despite more than 30 shots at goal they could score only once, through Friaca, two minutes into the second half. This was never going to be enough against a typically robust Uruguayan side. Inspired by the willowy Ghiggia, they began to carve huge holes in the Brazil back line and it was no surprise when Schiaffino glanced home the equaliser from a cross by Ghiggia. With the vast terraces screaming with anguish, Uruguay came again and, with eleven minutes remaining, Ghiggia's cross shot was misjudged by goalkeeper Barbosa and crossed the line for the decisive goal. It was a major upset, but Brazil had only themselves to blame. Their footballing philosophy was based on having the greatest attack in the world. Conceding a goal or two didn't matter as long as they were scoring six or seven at the other end. In 1950 they should have learned their lesson, yet this would not be the last time a Brazil side would lose a World Cup they should have won at a canter.

URUGUAY Maspoli, M Gonzalez, Tejera, Gambetta, Varela (c), Rodgriguez, Andrade, Ghiggia, Perez, Miguez, Schiaffino, Moran

BRAZIL Barbosa, Augusto (c), Juvenal, Bauer, Danilo, Bigode, Friaca, Zizinho, Ademir, Jair, Chico

---

1954

WEST GERMANY (2) 3 Morlock 10, Rahn 19, 85
HUNGARY (2) 2 Puskás 6, Czibor 8
Date 4 July 1954   **Venue** Wankdorf Stadium, Berne
Attendance 62,472   **Referee** Bill Ling (ENG)

A Hungary team which had laid waste to all before them for two years should have won the 1954 World Cup without breaking sweat, and until the final they appeared to be doing just that. But the Magic Magyars were about to learn that the competition is no respecter of class or form, and Puskás, Hidegkuti and co were put to the sword by a West German side that would provide a blueprint for efficiency and togetherness of purpose.

Having thrashed the Germans 8–3 in the group stage, at first it seemed like business as usual as Puskás and Czibor nonchalantly prodded Hungary 2–0 in front after just eight minutes. But this time the Germans, fielding six players from Kaiserslauten, were having none of it. The Magyars suddenly found their intricate triangles and first-time passing being stifled by German pressure. Morlock pounced on a rare defensive error to score after ten minutes, and after twenty the Germans were level through Rahn. In the second half Hungary attacked as if their lives depended on it, but Germany remained resolute. With five minutes left Shafer crossed the ball and defender Lantos could only head the ball weakly into the path of the predatory Rahn, who smashed it home. It was the end of a 32-match unbeaten run and earned Hungary the unwanted title of 'best team never to win the World Cup'.

WEST GERMANY Turek, Posipal, Kohlmeyer, Eckel, Liebrich, Mai, Rahn, Morlock, O Walter, F Walter (c), Shafer

HUNGARY Grosics, Buzansky, Lantos, Bozsik, Lorant, Zakarias, Czibor, Kocsis, Hidegkuti, Puskás (c), Toth

---

1958

BRAZIL (2) 5 Vava 9, 32, Pelé 55, 90, Zagallo 68
SWEDEN (1) 2 Liedholm 4, Simonsson 79
Date 29 June 1958 **Venue** Rasunda Stadium, Stockholm
Attendance 49,737 **Referee** Maurice Guigue (FRA)

It was eight years since Brazil had flopped so ignominiously against Uruguay, and they were determined that this time they would put matters right. And, although they scored after just four minutes, Sweden were never in the hunt against a side brimming with talent such as Didi, Vava, Garrincha and Pelé. The old Brazilian adage of attack being the best form of defence proved irresistible as Garrincha and Vava combined twice to shred the Swedish defence and give the South Americans the lead after 32 minutes. Ten minutes after the interval it was all over: Pelé, just seventeen years old, took a cross from Nilton Santos on his chest, flipped the ball over Gustavsson with his thigh, and drilled the ball past Svensson as it came down. Zagallo hit a fourth on 68 minutes and although Simonsson clipped home a second for Sweden after 79 minutes it did

nothing to stop the Brazilian juggernaut. In the dying seconds, Pelé effortlessly
backheeled the ball to Zagallo before running into the box to meet the cross.
His header looped over the helpless Svensson, leaving the goalkeeper wrapped
around his own post. It was an image which summed up Brazil's superiority on
a spectacular day when every component of their supercharged engine ran to
its full potential.

BRAZIL Gylmar, D Santos, N Santos, Zito, Bellini (c), Orlando, Garrincha,
Didi, Vava, Pelé, Zagallo

SWEDEN Svensson, Bergmark, Axbom, Borjesson, Gustavsson, Parling, Hamrin,
Gren, Simonsson, Liedholm (c), Skoglund

1962

BRAZIL (1) 3 Amarildo 16, Zito 69, Vava 78
CZECHOSLOVAKIA (1) 1 Masopust 14
Date 17 June 1962   **Venue** Nacional Stadium, Santiago
Attendance 68,679   **Referee** Nikolai Latyshev (USSR)

Although never as emphatic as their win against Sweden in 1958, Brazil
comfortably retained the World Cup against a limited Czech side that had held
the champions to a goalless draw in the group stage but could not suppress
them a second time. Brazil began the final in customary fashion, by conceding
an early goal. But, as usual, they equalised in a matter of minutes through
Amarildo. After that, it was one-way traffic; the only surprise being that it
took the Brazilians until the 69th minute to score again, Zito heading home
Amarildo's clever cross. Even without the injured Pelé, Brazil's firepower
was far too strong for the Czechs, and ten minutes later the irrepressible Vava
rounded it off with a simple tap-in after keeper Schrojf had dropped the ball.
With their two consecutive World Cup wins, Brazil were taking the game to
previously unexplored levels – and the best was yet to come.

BRAZIL Gylmar, D Santos, N Santos, Zito, Mauro (c), Zozimo, Garrincha, Didi, Vava, Amarildo, Zagallo
CZECHOSLOVAKIA Schroijf, Tichy, Novak (c), Pluskal, Popluhar, Masopust, Pospichal, Scherer, Kadraba, Kvasnak, Jelinek

---

1966
ENGLAND (1) (2) 4 Hurst 19, 100, 119, Peters 78
WEST GERMANY (1) (2) 2 (AET) Haller 13, Weber 89
Date 30 July 1966   **Venue** Wembley Stadium, London
Attendance 93,802   **Referee** Gottfried Dienst (SWI)

Having underperformed in their previous World Cup tournaments England failed to set this one alight until the latter stages. Fortunately, they were keeping the best till last. In front of 93,000 fans at Wembley Alf Ramsey's men showed reserves of stamina, resolve and courage that were previously thought to be the sole preserves of their opponents, West Germany.

Things couldn't have started worse for England. After thirteen minutes, Wilson made a hash of an innocuous-looking cross from Held. The ball fell to Haller who drilled it home from the edge of the penalty area. Six minutes later, England's West Ham connection combined for the first time. Using a move that had been perfected on the training ground at Upton Park, Bobby Moore clipped a quick free kick into the box where his Hammers teammate Geoff Hurst – a replacement for the injured arch-predator Jimmy Greaves – had drifted in unmarked to head the ball home.

For an hour the game was attritional. There were few chances, neither side willing to make the mistake that might cost them the match and the World Cup. Then, 78 minutes in, England won a corner. Alan Ball floated it in, Hurst's shot from the edge of the box was blocked, and Martin Peters was on hand to smash it into the net from just seven yards. It should have been all over then – but the Germans, marshalled by Schulz, Hottges and the youngster

Beckenbauer, did not believe in surrender. With less than a minute remaining, Jack Charlton was harshly penalised and when Emmerich hammered the free kick into the box, the ball pinballed to the near post where Weber was lurking to put it into the back of the net.

It was extra time for the first time since 1934, and it belonged to Geoff Hurst. Ten minutes in, the indefatigable Ball got the better of Emmerich on the right and crossed long from the corner flag. Hurst controlled the ball, swivelled and struck it with venom against the underside of the crossbar. Forty years on, debate still rages as to whether the ball crossed the line, but what matters is that Azerbaijani linesman Tofik Bakhramov thought it had. England were ahead again, and this time it was a sucker punch from which even the Germans could not recover. The game was won long before Hurst latched onto Bobby Moore's through ball and smashed it into the net from 20 yards.

England were World Champions at last, and they had won the trophy the hard way. Few would deny them their moment of glory.

ENGLAND Banks, Cohen, Wilson, Stiles, J Charlton, Moore (c), Ball, Hurst, R Charlton, Hunt, Peters

WEST GERMANY Tilkowski, Hottges, Schnellinger, Beckenbauer, Schulz, Weber, Held, Haller, Seeler (c), Overath, Emmerich

---

1970

BRAZIL (1) 4 Pelé 18, Gerson 66, Jairzinho 71, Carlos Alberto 86
ITALY (1) 1 Boninsegna 37
Date 21 June 1970 **Venue** Azteca Stadium, Mexico City
Attendance 107,412 **Referee** Rudi Glockner (East Germany)

In 1962 Brazil had been unstoppable. Now they were simply awesome. Fielding what many still believe to be the greatest team ever assembled for a World Cup finals, they annihilated a strong Italy with a verve and style which has not been seen before or since.

For once it was Brazil who got the early goal, and inevitably it was Pelé who scored it. Aged 29 and making his World Cup swansong, the 5ft 9in genius seemed to defy gravity as he leapt to meet Rivelino's cross in the 18th minute. A split-second later the ball was in the back of the net: it is doubtful whether goalkeeper Albertosi even saw it. Yet despite their virtuosity, Brazil were still susceptible to defensive howlers – and on 37 minutes, a lazy backheel by Clodoaldo allowed Boninsegna in for a goal which Italy scarcely deserved.

No matter: the equaliser simply made the destruction which followed in the second half all the more spectacular. Gerson and Jairzinho scored after Pelé had had a goal disallowed and Rivelino had hit the bar with a free kick. Then, with four minutes left, Clodoaldo held off several challenges in his own half before feeding Jairzinho on the left. The ball came to Pelé on the edge of the box and his leisurely but perfectly paced square pass was met full-on by the skipper Carlos Alberto, whose right foot shot nearly ripped the netting out of the ground.

It was a stunning climax to a dazzling tournament for Brazil. They had now won the World Cup three times, but even though they would go on to win it on two further occasions nothing would compare to this.

BRAZIL Felix, Carlos Alberto (c), Everaldo, Clodoaldo, Brito, Piazza, Jairzinho, Gerson, Tostao, Pelé, Rivelino

ITALY Albertosi, Burgnich, Facchetti (c), Bertini [Juliano 74], Rosato, Cera, Domenghini, Mazzola, Boninsegna [Rivera 84], De Sisti, Riva

---

1974

WEST GERMANY (2) 2 Breitner pen 25, Muller 43
HOLLAND (1) 1 Neeskens pen 2
Date 7 July 1974   **Venue** Olympic Stadium, Munich
Attendance 77,833   **Referee** Jack Taylor (ENG)

World Cup finals had a tendency towards early goals, but none as early as the one that broke the deadlock in the 1974 final between hosts West Germany and Holland. Barely two minutes had gone when Dutch maestro Johan Cruyff's mazy run towards the German goal was ended when he was upended in the area by Uli Hoeness. English referee Jack Taylor pointed to the spot and Neeskens coolly sent Sepp Maier the wrong way. It was a sensational start and one which stunned the capacity crowd at Munich's impressive Olympic Stadium.

The goal should have been the springboard for the superb Dutch side, inspired by Cruyff, to go on to win their first World Cup – yet the side who had lit up the tournament with their magnificent brand of Total Football seemed uncertain how to proceed, whether to defend their lead or go all out to humiliate the hated Germans. In the end, the chink of light they offered was exploited to the full by their pragmatic opponents.

With Vogts patrolling Cruyff, the Dutch seemed bereft of ideas, almost panic-stricken. The Germans came back strongly, and after 25 minutes Holzenbein went sprawling in the box under Jansen's challenge and Taylor once again pointed to the spot. Breitner hammered the ball home and suddenly it was the Germans who were in the ascendant.

Two minutes before the break, Bonhof left Ari Haan for dead and clipped the ball back across from the by-line to where the unmistakable figure of Gerd Muller was lurking. At first it seemed Muller had let the chance escape – but almost with his back to goal, the ace marksman swivelled and planted the ball past the static Jongbloed. In the second half the Germans gave Holland an object lesson in how to defend a lead. Captain Beckenbauer, in his third World Cup, was outstanding, as was Vogts, in stemming the orange tide of pressure. Maier made a great save from Neeskens, but with Cruyff neutralised the threat was minimised.

After the pyrotechnics of 1970 it was not pretty – but it was mightily effective. The Germans had the honour of being the first team to lift the newly minted FIFA World Cup Trophy.

WEST GERMANY Maier, Vogts, Breitner, Bonhof, Schwarzenbeck, Beckenbauer (c), Grabowski, Hoeness, Muller, Overath, Holzenbein

HOLLAND Jongbloed, Suurbier, Krol, Jansen, Rijsbergen [de Jong 68], Haan, Rep, Neeskens, van Hanegen, Cruyff (c), Rensenbrink [R van der Kerkhof HT]

1978

ARGENTINA (1) (1) 3 Kempes 37, 104, Bertoni 115
HOLLAND (0) (1) 1 (AET) Nanninga 82
Date 25 June 1978   **Venue** Monumental Stadium, Buenos Aires
Attendance 76,609   **Referee** Sergio Gonella (ITA)

Just how badly Holland were affected by the pre-match shenanigans which
marred the 1978 final against Argentina is debatable, but the unnecessary
ten-minute delay while Rene van der Kerkhof was obliged to cover up the
protective cast on his wrist benefited no-one but the hosts. But then this was
always destined to be Argentina's year. Having survived an early onslaught by
the Dutch, the Argentines opened the scoring in the 37th minute when Ardiles
threaded a ball through to Kempes who prodded it past Jongbloed. After that,
the hosts sat back, content to commit a series of fouls and handballs safe in the
knowledge that the weak Italian referee would do nothing to punish them.

It is testament to the determination and skill of the Dutch that they not
only equalised – Nanninga heading home Rene van der Kerkhof's cross in the
82nd minute – but were denied a last-gasp victory when Resenbrink's shot
came back off the post.

In extra time the leggy Kempes struck again, galloping into the box and
scoring from a rebound of his own shot. Ten minutes later, Bertoni applied the
coup de grâce, as the weary Dutch failed to clear their lines. Argentina had won
the World Cup, but few friends. For the second successive time the trophy had
gone to the host nation, and for the second time the bridesmaids had been the
Dutch.

ARGENTINA Fillol, Olguin, Tarantini, Gallego, Galvan, Passarella (c), Bertoni,
Ardiles [Larosa 65], Luque, Kempes, Ortiz [Houseman 74]
HOLLAND Jongbloed, Krol (c), Brandts, Poortvliet, Jansen [Suurbier 72],
Haan, R van der Kerkhof, Neeskens, Rep [Nanninga 59], W van der Kerkhof,
Rensenbrink

1982

ITALY (0) 3 Rossi 56, Tardelli 68, Altobelli 80
WEST GERMANY (0) 1 Breitner 83
Date 11 July 1982   **Venue** Bernabeu Stadium, Madrid
Attendance 90,089   **Referee** Arnaldo Coelho (BRA)

Italy's convincing and wholly deserved win belied the fact that they had up until the second group stage been wholly unconvincing and deserving only of the first plane back to Rome. The moment of epiphany came against the favourites Brazil, when Paolo Rossi bagged a hat trick in a dramatic 3–2 win and suddenly anything seemed possible.

West Germany, meanwhile, had won few friends on their way to the final. They had adopted a physical approach, personified by the hulking former decathlete Hans Pieter Briegel in midfield and by goalkeeper Harald Schumacher's brutal assault on Battiston in the semi-final against France.

In the end, Briegel's chief contribution in the final was to give away a penalty after 24 minutes which Cabrini scuffed horribly wide. In the second half, he was chasing shadows as the nimble Conti and Tardelli increased the pressure to breaking point. Rossi continued his scoring spree with a close-range header on 56 minutes and then twelve minutes later Marco Tardelli's drive from the edge of the box was surpassed only by his impassioned goal celebration. The ragged Germans were beaten long before Altobelli rounded Schumacher to make it 3–0, but were still able to strike a note of defiance three minutes later when Breitner, in his third World Cup, became only the third player to score in two finals. The defeat was West Germany's first to a European country since 1978.

ITALY Zoff (c), Bergomi, Cabrini, Gentile, Oriali, Collovati, Scirea, Tardelli, Conti, Rossi, Graziani [Altobelli 7, Causio 89]
WEST GERMANY Schumacher, Kaltz, Briegel, B Forster, K-H Forster, Stielike, Littbarski, Dremmler [Hrubesch 62], Breitner, Fischer, Rummenigge (c) [H Muller 70]

1986

ARGENTINA (1) 3 Brown 23, Valdano 56, Burruchaga 85
WEST GERMANY (0) 2 Rummenigge 74, Voller 82
Date 29 June 1986 **Venue** Azteca Stadium, Mexico
Attendance 114,580 **Referee** Romualdo Arppi (Brazil)

West German coach Franz Beckenbauer admitted before the game that he
didn't have the players to win the title – but German football has always been
more about solidarity than individual flair, and in 1986 the Kaiser's men came
within a whisker of causing a major upset against Maradona's Argentina.

Indeed it has been argued that had it not been for an inexplicable lapse in
form by the consistently excellent Schumacher in the German goal, the game
might have been won easily.

As it was, two errors by the shaggy-haired keeper gave Argentina a 2–0
lead out of nothing. First he came and missed Burruchaga's free kick to allow
Brown to head into an empty net; then he dithered as Valdano burst through to
slot the ball past his right hand.

Two corners in eight minutes by Brehme brought the West Germans level. On
74 minutes Rummenigge, playing through injury, bundled the ball home at the back
post, then on 82 Voller got ahead of Pumpido's fists to divert the ball into the net.

Perhaps aware of Rummenigge's condition, Beckenbauer ordered his men
to go for the kill instead of playing for extra time. It was to be a fatal decision.
Maradona, largely anonymous until then, played a sublime defence-splitter to
put Buruchaga away. Once again Schumacher stayed on his line, and once again
he was forced to pick the ball out of the back of the net.

It was harsh on the Germans but, considering the 1986 tournament had
been a succession of Maradona masterclasses, the result seemed only fair.

ARGENTINA Pumpido, Cuciuffo, Olarticoechea, Enrique, Ruggeri, Brown,
Giusti, Battista, Burruchaga [Trobbiani 89], Maradona (c), Valdano
WEST GERMANY Schumacher, Berthold, Briegel, Jakobs, Forster, Eder,
Matthaus, Brehme, Allofs [Voller HT], Magath [Hoeness 61], Rummenigge (c)

1990

WEST GERMANY (0) 1 Brehme pen 84
ARGENTINA (0) 0
Date 8 July 1990   **Venue** Olympic Stadium, Rome
Attendance 73,603   **Referee** Edgardo Codesal (MEX)

Perhaps the World Cup was due for a stinker of a final. It certainly got it in 1990. In England, the exploits of Gazza and co earlier in the tournament tend to overshadow quite what a dismal, mean-spirited game this was.

Argentina were without four suspended players, and were deprived of two more when Monzon and Dezotti were sent off in the second half. Maradona, their inspiration four years earlier, was marked out of the game by the hulking Buchwald.

It made little difference. The Germans, who had scored only a single goal in their previous three matches, rarely came close through open play and the game would have surely drifted into extra time and most probably penalties had Sensini not brought Voller down in the box with six minutes to go.

One thing the West Germans had proved they were good at in this tournament was penalties (just ask England in the semi-finals), and Andreas Brehme duly converted the spot kick.

It was third time lucky for West Germany, and the last time they would compete as a divided nation. It was just a shame such a momentous occasion should turn out to be such a travesty of a football match.

WEST GERMANY Illgner, Berthold [Reuter 73], Brehme, Buchwald, Kohler, Augenthaler, Hassler, Matthaus (c), Littbarski, Voller, Klinsmann
ARGENTINA Goycochea, Simon, Sensini, Basualdo, Serrizuela, Ruggeri [Monzon HT], Burruchaga [Calderon 53], Troglio, Lorenzo, Maradona (c), Dezotti
Sent off Monzon 64, Dezotti 86

1994

BRAZIL 0
ITALY 0 Brazil 3–2 pens (AET)
Penalty shoot-out Baresi shot over, Marcio Santos saved, Albertini 1–0, Romario 1–1, Evani 2–1, Branco 2–2, Massaro saved, Dunga 2–3, R Baggio shot over
Date 17 July 1994 **Venue** Rose Bowl, Pasadena
Attendance 94,194 **Referee** Sandor Puhl (HUN)

After the horrors of the 1990 final, we were due something special – and who better to provide it than Brazil and Italy, old adversaries and combatants in the legendary 1970 final?

But the game was another washout, the first to be decided on a penalty shoot-out. What chances there were could be counted on one hand, and most of them were for Brazil. Mazinho should have scored when Pagliuca saved Branco's free kick, Romario missed an open goal and Pagliuca fumbled Mauro Silva's shot onto the post. For Italy, Roberto Baggio should have scored when put through against Taffarel, but his weary shot betrayed a striker who was both unfit and out of form.

Worse was to come for Baggio as he stepped up to take his penalty. Needing to score to level the scores at 3–3 and keep the shoot-out alive, the pony-tailed Juventus star blazed his shot high over the bar. The trophy was Brazil's again after 24 years.

BRAZIL Taffarel, Jorginho [Cafu 21], Branco, Mazinho, Aldair, Marcio Santos, Mauro Silva, Dunga (c), Romario, Bebeto, Zinho [Viola 105]
ITALY Pagliuca, Mussi [Apolloni 34], Benarrivo, Berti, Maldini, Baresi (c), Donadoni, Albertini, Massaro, R Baggio, D Baggio [Evani 94]

1998

FRANCE (2) 3 Zidane 27, 44, Petit 90
BRAZIL (0) 0
Date 12 July 1998   **Venue** Stade de France, Paris
Attendance 75,000   **Referee** Said Belqola (MOR)

After dominating European football for more than two years, France won
their first World Cup on home soil and in some style. Architect of their victory
was the incomparable Zinedine Zidane, who throughout the tournament had
shown a level of skill and technique worthy of the great Brazilians of the past.

By comparison, Brazil's own maestro, Ronaldo, was in disarray. Afflicted
by a mystery illness on the day of the game, the predatory striker was initially
withdrawn from the starting line-up, only to be reinstated just 45 minutes
before kickoff.

Quite simply it was one-way traffic. Guivarc'h should have scored twice
in the opening minutes as the French laid siege to the Brazilian goal, and had
Djorkaeff made contact with his head rather than his shoulder to a near-post
cross Taffarel would have had no chance. As it was, the French crowd had to
wait 27 minutes for the first goal. Petit's perfectly flighted corner was met
powerfully by Zidane whose header crashed into the back of the net.

With Brazil reeling against the ropes, France went in for the kill. In injury
time at the end of the first half, Zidane struck again, stooping to head home
Djorkaeff's corner from the right.

In the second half, Ronaldo stirred – but was clearly out of sorts. Put
through against Barthez, he fluffed the sort of chance he would normally have
gobbled up and the goalkeeper collected easily. All around the pitch, Brazilian
heads dropped. Even when Desailly was sent off for scything down Cafu after
67 minutes, the South Americans were unable to raise their game.

The *coup de grâce* came in the final seconds of the match when Petit raced
clear and coolly slotted the ball past Taffarel to make it 3–0 and send the whole
of France into paroxysms of delight.

FRANCE Barthez, Thuram, Leboeuf, Desailly, Lizarazu, Karembeu [Boghossian 57], Deschamps (c), Zidane, Petit, Djorkaeff (Vieira 76), Guivarc'h [Dugarry 65]
BRAZIL Taffarel, Cafu, Aldair, Junior Baiano, Roberto Carlos, Leonardo [Denilson 46], Cesar Sampaio [Edmundo 74], Dunga (c), Rivaldo, Ronaldo, Bebeto

---

2002

BRAZIL (0) 2 Ronaldo 67, 79
GERMANY (0) 0
Date: 30 June 2002 **Venue** International Stadium, Yokohama
Attendance 69,029 **Referee** Pierluigi Collina (ITA)

Four years after being waylaid by a mystery illness, Ronaldo was back on the biggest stage in football – and this time he did not disappoint. Two goals – the first a poacher's special, the second a piece of finishing excellence – gave Brazil their fifth World Cup trophy and squashed any speculation that the South Americans were a spent force in world football.

It was Germany, appearing in their fifth final in 18 years, who started the brighter. Inspired by Bernd Schneider, they pressurised the Brazilian goal without ever creating a clear-cut chance, and for a while the final seemed to be heading the same way as it had in France four years earlier. Brazil, though, looked sharp on the break. Twice Ronaldo was sent clear by the livewire Ronaldinho, only to blow the chance on both occasions. Germany's failure to convert pressure into goals cost them dear in the second half. On 67 minutes a speculative shot from Rivaldo was spilled by the usually rock-solid Kahn in the German goal, and Ronaldo was on hand to bang home the rebound.

Twelve minutes later, Kahn was helpless in the face of some overdue Brazilian magic. Kleberson broke down the right and squared the ball to Rivaldo. Rivaldo stepped over the ball, allowing it to run through to Ronaldo on the edge of the box. There was still much to do, but the striker's finish was emphatic and unstoppable.

Brazil were World Champions again and Ronaldo had silenced the doubters after four years.

BRAZIL Marcos, Edmilson, Lucio, Roque Junior, Cafu (c), Kleberson, Gilberto, Roberto Carlos, Ronaldinho [Juninho Paulista 85], Rivaldo, Ronaldo [Denilson 90]

GERMANY Kahn(c), Linke, Ramelow, Metzelder, Frings, Schneider, Jeremies [Asamoah 77], Hamann, Bode [Ziege 84], Neuville, Klose [Bierhoff 73]

2006

FRANCE 1 Zidane 7
ITALY 1 Materazzi 19
Italy 5–3 pens (AET)
Penalty shoot-out Pirlo 1–0, Wiltord 1–1, Materazzi 2–1, Trezeguet hit the crossbar, De Rossi 3–1, Abidal 3–2, Del Piero 4–2, Sagnol 4–3, Grosso 5–3.
Date 9 July 2006   **Venue** Olympiastadion, Berlin
Attendance 69,000   **Referee** Horacio Elizondo (ARG)

The 2006 final will forever be remembered for all the wrong reasons. A moment of madness from one of the most talented players ever to take to the pitch marred an encounter in which both teams initially attacked with gusto, playing with much more open styles than pundits had predicted.

There was excitement early on, with both sides scoring early in the first half. France were awarded a controversial penalty in the 7th minute when Malouda fell in the box after Materazzi appeared to catch his foot. Inevitably, playing in his last match before his official retirement, France captain Zinedine Zidane stepped up to the spot to convert with a casual strike that somewhat fortuitously glanced in off the underside of the crossbar. Italy rallied however and equalised in the 19th minute when Milan's Andrea Pirlo whipped in a corner from the right. Materazzi thumped a header past Fabien Barthez, atoning for his earlier error. The Italian would have a bigger part still to play though.

France found it difficult to deal with set pieces, and indeed, Materazzi saw a second header from another Pirlo corner cleared off the line by Lilian Thuram, before Luca Toni nodded onto the bar – again from a Pirlo corner. Having just held on, France emerged revitalised for the second half, with Thierry Henry at the centre of things. In the 53rd minute Malouda again went down in the box after a Zambrotta tackle, but no penalty was given. Somewhat against the run of play Italy managed to put the ball in the net for a second time; Luca Toni heading in a Pirlo free kick, but the goal was disallowed for offside. At the other end Henry's running continued to be effective and Buffon showed his quality in saving a snap-shot. Still 1–1 after 90 minutes, the game entered extra time and Malouda was only dispossessed by a last-ditch Cannavaro tackle before Franck Ribery shot wide and Buffon crucially tipped a Zidane header over.

Then, with 10 minutes left of extra time, Zidane and Materazzi looked to exchange words after some shirt-pulling. Having initially walked away, Zidane then stopped, turned around and headbutted Materazzi full in the chest. Materazzi dropped to the floor and although play was halted, Argentinian referee Horacio Elizondo did not appear to have seen the incident. Some minutes elapsed before Zidane was shown a red card in the 110th minute, the referee having apparently been informed of the headbutt by the fourth official via his headset. Zidane trudged from the pitch, ignoring the World Cup trophy displayed next to the tunnel – a picture that dominated the sporting papers the following day. A shell-shocked France managed to hold on without their captain to take the final to penalties.

All five Italy players scored their spot kicks, and France ultimately lost out when David Trezeguet's penalty hit the crossbar. Fabio Grosso coolly slotted home to make the score 5–3 and secure the World Cup for Italy, the nation's fourth overall.

The fallout from the Zidane incident was huge, and both players were ultimately fined by FIFA. The media clamoured to know what Materazzi had said to Zidane; it later transpired that Zidane had firstly responded to the Italian's shirt-pulling by remarking, 'If you want my shirt, I will give it to you afterwards', and Materazzi retorted, 'Preferisco la puttana di tua sorella' ('I prefer the whore that is your sister'). A nasty insult, certainly, but, the world questioned, did it merit the headbutt that tainted Zidane's incomparable career and may have cost France the World Cup?

FRANCE Barthez, Sagnol, Thuram, Gallas, Abidal, Vieira [Alou Diarra 56], Makelele, Ribery [Trezeguet 100], Zidane (c), Malouda, Henry [Wiltord 107]

ITALY Buffon, Zambrotta, Cannavaro (c), Materazzi, Grosso, Gattuso, Pirlo, Camoranesi [Del Piero 86], Perrotta [De Rossi 61], Totti [Iaquinta 61], Toni

---

2010

HOLLAND 0
SPAIN 1 Iniesta 116
Date 11 July 2010   **Venue** Soccer City, Johannesburg
Attendance 84,490   **Referee** Howard Webb (ENG)

The final everyone wanted to see was Brazil vs Spain, the South American masters against the European champions, languid samba soccer against quick-fire tiki-taka precision. But when Brazil were despatched by Holland in the quarter-finals, the prospect of an all-European final was suddenly on the cards. The much-anticipated clash duly materialised, with the Dutch seeing off a spirited Uruguay 3–2 and the Spanish continuing on their serene progress to the final with a 1–0 win over the Germans in the semis. But with the scene set, not only by a spectacular closing ceremony but an appearance by Nelson Mandela, what transpired on the pitch that night in the packed Soccer City stadium in Johannesburg was both a crushing disappointment for football fans of any persuasion and a display of petulance, gamesmanship and outright cheating that could justifiably be accused of bringing the game into disrepute.

Remarkably, Spain and Holland had never before met in the final stages of a World or European tournament. Indeed, in the previous 90 years they'd only met nine times, and one of those occasions was at the 1920 Olympics. Another nugget for the statisticians is that this would be the first time since 1978, when Holland lined up against Argentina, that the final would be contested by two teams who had never won the tournament.

From the first whistle it was clear that the Dutch were in no mood to indulge the dainty footwork of the Spanish. Nor, it would appear, were they interested in playing any sort of football themselves. Instead, they set about bludgeoning their opponents off the ball and out of the game. The Spanish understandably reacted in kind, and the result was a toxic confrontation in which there were a record 14 yellow cards, a sending-off, and a single extra-time goal which resulted from one of the very few moments of sublime football in the match.

The first 90 minutes is best forgotten. Indeed the only highlight amid the constant niggling and fouling was an outrageous studs-up assault on Spain's Xabi Alonso by Nigel de Jong, which English referee Howard Webb somehow adjudged was worthy only of a yellow card. Justice was seen to be done in the 82nd minute, however, when Arjen Robben, put through one-on-one against Iker Casillas, was denied the winning goal by the splendid Spanish goalkeeper.

If ever a match could have done without an extra 30 minutes it was this one. But at least at the end of it the tournament had worthy winners. With four minutes to go and 10-man Holland (Webb having finally sent off Holland's John Heitinga) hanging on for penalties, some delightful play on the edge of the box provided Andres Iniesta with a chance to drive the ball past Stekelenberg and into the net.

Spanish joy at the final whistle was matched by almost universal condemnation of the brutish Dutch tactics, with even the great Johan Cruyff describing Holland's contribution to the final as 'ugly, vulgar and anti-football'. It was a sad end to a joyful tournament.

HOLLAND Stekelenberg, van der Wiel, Heitinga, Mathijsen, van Bronkhorst (c) [Braafheid 105], van Bommel, de Jong [van der Vaart 99], Robben, Sneijder, Kuyt [Elia 71], van Persie

SPAIN Casillas (c), Ramos, Pique, Puyol, Capdevila, Busquets, Alonso [Fabregas 87], Xavi, Iniesta, Pedro [Navas 60], Villa [Torres 106]

MEXICO OR BUST

In 1970 Jimmy Greaves was judged too old, at 30, for a place in the England World Cup squad and was left at home by Sir Alf Ramsey. Greaves, however, had other ideas, and together with rally driver Tony Falls he entered the inaugural World Cup Rally Championship, a race from Wembley to Mexico City covering 16,241 miles and crossing 25 countries. They made it in just under a month. The race, strangely enough, was started by Sir Alf Ramsey.

DOGGED GREAVES

Despite being one of the finest marksmen in the domestic game and scoring 44 goals in 57 appearances for England, Jimmy Greaves's World Cup exploits are perhaps best forgotten as, having secured a place in Alf Ramsey's 1966 team, he was injured in the last first-round game against France and, having recovered, was then left out of the final in favour of Geoff Hurst. Indeed Greavesie's finest moment in the white of England may well have come in 1962 during a match against Brazil in Vina Del Mar. Trailing 3–1 and heading out of the World Cup, England's mood was lightened slightly when a dog ran onto the pitch and proceeded to evade all attempts to capture it. Quick as a flash, Greaves got down on all fours in the centre circle and, by growling at it, succeeded in startling the dog long enough to grab it. It was perhaps symptomatic of Greavesie's England career that, as he carried it to the touchline, the dog urinated all over his England shirt.

WINGLESS WONDERS?

Alf Ramsey's 1966 England side became known as the Wingless Wonders, but in fact Ramsey used wingers right up until the quarter-final against Argentina.

ENGLAND PLAYERS WHO PLAYED IN THE 1966 TOURNAMENT – BUT NOT IN THE FINAL

Terry Paine (vs Mexico)
Ian Callaghan (vs France)
John Connelly (vs Uruguay)
Jimmy Greaves (vs Uruguay, Mexico, France)

THE LONG AND THE SHORT OF IT

The Group C match between Brazil and China in 2002 featured that particular World Cup's tallest and shortest players – Brazilian midfielder Juninho Paulista at 5ft 4ins (1.67m) and Chinese goalkeeper Jin Jiang, 6ft 4ins (1.98m).

TRAGIC END

Georgi Asparoukhov and Stojan Kotkov, who played together for Bulgaria in the 1966 World Cup, were both killed in the same car crash in 1971.

RATTIN GETS HIS MARCHING ORDERS

West German referee Rudolf Kreitlein had already booked five players during the stormy World Cup quarter-final between England and Argentina in 1966 when, with nearly half an hour gone, his patience finally snapped. During that time, Argentine skipper Antonio Rattin had spat in front of him, disputed every decision made against his side and committed a series of blatant fouls. Kreitlein, who had already cautioned Rattin, now sent him off. Or at least he tried to. Rattin refused to go, claiming – nonsensically – that he required an interpreter. Meanwhile teammate Albrecht signalled that if the captain was going then the rest of the side should go with him. The rest of the team, meanwhile, had surrounded the referee and there would be eight minutes of mayhem before Rattin finally left the pitch. Even then it took a quiet word from the police to persuade him to move away from the touchline and begin a long, leisurely walk around the perimeter to the changing rooms.

VILLAIN OF THE PIECE

Having already had their captain Antonio Rattin sent off, Argentina cemented their reputation as pantomime villains of the 1966 World Cup after Geoff Hurst gave England a 77th minute lead at Wembley. A small boy ran onto the pitch to congratulate the West Ham striker – but left in tears after Argentine winger Mas clipped him round the ear.

NO LAUGHING MATTER

Dick Nanninga of Holland became the first substitute to be sent off in a World Cup tournament when he was given his marching orders in the group match against West Germany in 1978. His offence? Laughing at Uruguayan referee Ramon Barreto. Nanninga would return in the final and score Holland's only goal against Argentina, again as substitute.

TWO GOALS FOR ERNIE

The game between Holland and Italy in the second group stage of the 1978 World Cup will be remembered for Arie Haan's 40-yard thunderbolt which beat Dino Zoff off the post. But the match was fairly eventful for Haan's teammate Ernie Brandts, who put Italy in front with an own goal after nineteen minutes, only to make amends by equalising with a 20-yarder four minutes after the break. The second goal meant he was the first player ever to score for both sides in a World Cup tournament.

FOUL PLAY

There is no love lost between Brazil and Argentina. In their 1978 clash, there were no fewer than seventeen fouls in the first ten minutes. Amazingly no-one was sent off as the two sides ground out a dour 0–0 draw.

LUQUE PLAYS ON

Despite the death of his brother in a car crash midway through the 1978 tournament, Argentina's Leopoldo Luque decided to play on in his honour.

LONG RANGE

In the 1978 finals in Argentina, the four goals conceded by Italy's Dino Zoff were all shots hit from outside the penalty area.

GOAL-CRAZY GERMANS

West Germany were firm favourites, along with Brazil, to win the 1982 World Cup in Spain. Not only were they the reigning European champions, but they had won all eight of their qualifying games, scoring 33 goals and conceding just three. In their first match of the tournament, they lost 2–1 to 1000–1 outsiders Algeria.

TEUTONIC REVENGE?

There were red faces all round when Algeria beat West Germany in Group 2 of the 1982 finals. But the Germans were to have their revenge in the most controversial of circumstances eight days later. Algeria led Chile 3–0 at half time in their last match and, had the score remained the same, only a 4–3 win or better against Austria would have saved the Germans from ignominious elimination. Agonisingly, Chile scored two in the second half – which meant a 1–0 win for West Germany would suffice for them and Austria to proceed on goal difference at Algeria's expense. Because the Algeria match kicked off earlier, the Germans and the Austrians knew this as well. And when Hrubesch scored after eleven minutes, the game deteriorated to the level of a friendly training match, with neither side exerting themselves or showing much interest in scoring again. Furious Algerian fans showed their displeasure by waving banknotes through the wire fencing as the two European sides tamely played out time. Afterwards rumours were rife that the match had been fixed, that the West Germans had reached an agreement with their neighbours to get Algeria eliminated. The counter-argument was that Austria had a long-standing grudge with Germany and therefore had no reason to let them through. Whatever the truth, the match left a sour taste in the mouth as Algeria, who had thrilled the neutrals, were knocked out on goal difference.

Algeria understandably complained to FIFA that the game had been fixed, and called for both sides to be disqualified. Showing a sadly typical lack of backbone, FIFA declined to act. Austria, having spurned a great opportunity to dump their great European rivals out of the World Cup, were themselves expelled in the next stage. West Germany went on to the final, where they were well beaten 3–1 by Italy.

IRISH EYES SMILING

When Patrick Healy of Coleraine came on as a 77th minute substitute for Northern Ireland in their 1982 group match against Honduras he became the only Irish player in World Cup history still to be playing for an Irish club.

SOLIDARITY

There was more at stake than just a football match when Poland played USSR in 1982. Back home the Poles, in the form of trade union Solidarity, were protesting vociferously against their Soviet overlords – and in Barcelona's

Nou Camp stadium dozens of Solidarnosc flags were draped on the terraces. That was until the Spanish police waded in with batons raised to remove the banners, apparently at the request of Soviet television. It was a shameful incident and one which only served to raise the profile of the union to the watching millions. The game itself ended in a tame 0–0 draw.

KEV AND TREV

Injured before the tournament, Kevin Keegan and Trevor Brooking were finally pressed into emergency service 63 minutes into England's crunch match against hosts Spain in 1982. Needing to win by at least two goals, Brooking fired a shot straight at goalkeeper Arkonada and Keegan missed a far-post header ('No excuses – I should have buried it.'). England were out and neither Keegan nor Brooking would play for their country again. Sadly the World Cup careers of these brilliant players amounted to just 27 minutes.

TV INFLUENCE

The influence of TV companies in shaping World Cup tournaments was never more in evidence than in Mexico in 1986. It was ordered that matches had to end precisely after 90 minutes to fit in with advertising schedules, while kickoffs were brought forward to lunchtime – the hottest part of the day – to enable matches to be screened at convenient times in Europe. Chief culprit for this lunatic scheduling – which would be repeated in the USA in 1994 – was Guillermo Canedo, a FIFA vice-president who also happened to be a leading executive with an independent Mexican television company responsible for networking the coverage. When asked about the prohibitively high ticket prices, Canedo replied that 'people always have TV'.

THE RIGHT CHOICE

Enzo Scifo was qualified to play for Italy in the 1986 World Cup, but instead chose to play for his native Belgium. It proved to be the right choice, as Scifo, one of the stars of the tournament, guided the unfancied Belgians through to the last four while Italy failed even to make the quarter-finals.

NOBBY'S NIGHTMARE

England cruised to victory in their final 1966 Group 1 game against France. But while Roger Hunt celebrated his 28th birthday by scoring both goals, teammate Nobby Stiles had a match to forget. Booked for a foul and then extremely lucky not to have been sent off for a late challenge on Simon, his misery was compounded when he was accidentally knocked flying by the referee. Indeed there were many FA officials who wanted Stiles dropped from the team. Fortunately, Alf Ramsey held firm – and the rest is history.

LONG SERVANT

At the age of 37 Mexico's goalkeeper Antonio Carbajal was recalled to the side for their final 1966 group match against Uruguay. Remarkably it was his fifth World Cup finals, a record at the time – and he celebrated by keeping a clean sheet.

THE LONG WAIT

Ian Callaghan of Liverpool played only once in the 1966 World Cup finals, against Mexico. The next time he played for England was in 1977, a gap of 11 years 59 days – still the England record.

SWISS SHOOT THEMSELVES IN THE FOOT

Having arrived at the 1966 World Cup as rank outsiders, the Swiss did
nothing to help their own cause by suspending their two best players, Werner
Leimgruber and Jakob Kuhn. The two players had broken a curfew and were
sidelined on the eve of the first match against Germany – a match which they
subsequently lost 5–0. It was to be Switzerland's last appearance in a World
Cup until 1994.

NOT A NATIONAL

Eusebio, star of the Portugal side in 1966, was born in Mozambique.

UNPARALLELED ADEMIR

Eight years before the arrival of Pelé, Brazilian football was in thrall to another
gifted genius. Ademir entranced the opposition in 1950, and none more so than
Sweden against whom he scored four brilliant goals in a 7–1 rout. Pick of the bunch
was his third, in which he trapped the ball between his ankles and jumped over
the diving goalkeeper before slotting it coolly into the back of the net.

UP STEPS O'LEARY

On a night of almost unbearable tension in Genoa, the Republic of Ireland
and Romania went to penalties in a match to decide who would progress
to the 1990 quarter-finals. With the scores tied at 4–4, veteran keeper Pat
Bonner dived to his right to save Timofte's timid kick – which meant that the
fate of the Irish lay with defender David O'Leary, a man who had never taken
a penalty in competitive football. O'Leary stepped up and calmly slotted
the spot kick, sparking wild scenes of jubilation among the Irish fans and
guaranteeing their highest-ever World Cup finish.

MUSICAL URUGUAY

Schubert Gambetta played in defence for Uruguay in 1950, while Mozart Javier was a midfielder in a qualifying match against England in 1977.

QUITE A DEBUT

Ruben Moran is the only player to make his international debut in a World Cup final. He appeared on the wing for Uruguay in the deciding group match in 1950 and helped his team to a famous 2–1 win over the much-fancied Brazilians in Rio.

FAULTLESS WYSSLING DISPLAY

Two of the referees in the 1954 World Cup finals were Paul Wyssling of Switzerland and Charlie Faultless of Scotland.

LEG MASSAGE

Having already lost 12–0 to the same side at the 1952 Olympics, the South Koreans knew it was going to be a long afternoon when Hungary's Puskás scored after just 11 minutes of their Group 2 match at the 1954 World Cup in Switzerland. When Peter Palotas slid home the seventh with thirteen minutes still remaining, it was too much for South Korea's 37-year-old midfielder Chung Nam-sik, who sat down exhausted on the pitch. Fortunately, Hungarian defender Jeno Buzanszky was on hand to revive the veteran with a timely leg massage. It didn't stop the rout, however – Palotas and Puskás scored twice more to complete a 9–0 hammering for the Koreans.

GERMAN STUDS

In 1954, the West Germans were the first team to use screw-in studs.

A GREAT RECORD ENDS

West Germany's 3–2 win over Hungary in the 1954 final brought to an end a run of 29 matches without defeat. During that time, Hungary – with Puskás, Hidegkuti and Kocsis to the fore – had beaten Czechoslovakia 5–0, Italy 5–1, Sweden 6–2, South Korea 12–0 and 9–0, and England 6–3 and 7–1. They would never again reach such a pinnacle. Two years later, the Soviet Union invaded Hungary, and what remained of the Magic Magyars scattered to clubs elsewhere in Europe.

LAGER LOUT

Helmut Rahn of West Germany who had scored twice in the 1954 final aganst Hungary also scored two goals in his country's 3–1 win over Argentina in the opening game of the 1958 World Cup in Sweden and went on to score six in total as the Germans progressed as far as the semi-finals. But the influential striker only made the squad at the very last after coach Sepp Herberger persuaded him to lose weight by reducing his lager intake.

ITALIAN AT HEART

Mazzola – whose real name was José Altafini – played up front for Brazil in the 1958 World Cup finals, and took his name from the great Italian Valentino Mazzola, who was killed in the 1949 air crash that wiped out the entire Torino squad. The nineteen-year-old clearly had an affinity for Italy because he moved there after the World Cup and played for them in the 1962 tournament. Valentino's son, Sandro Mazzola, played in three World Cups for Italy.

WRONG DIAGNOSIS

For their final group game against the USSR in 1958, Brazilian coach Vicente Feola decided to blood two promising untested players, one a teenager. Before the game, he asked the team psychiatrist Joao Carvalhaes what he thought of them. The first, said Carvalhaes, was 'too young, too infantile' and the other 'so unsophisticated that including him in the team would be a disaster'. Feola disagreed and picked the tyros anyway. Their names? Pelé and Garrincha.

OUT OF CONTROL

The award for weakest refereeing performance of all time surely goes to Albert Dusch of West Germany, who was put in charge of the 1962 group match between USSR and Yugoslavia. There was little love lost between the two sides, as became apparent from the start when both sides launched into each other with a series of fouls. At the very least a warning might have calmed the situation, but Dusch did nothing. The situation became farcical when USSR's Dubinsky was hospitalised with a broken leg following a horrendous tackle by Yugoslav skipper Muhamed Mujic. The challenge was so bad, Mujic was later sent home by his own management – but again Dusch did nothing. Nor did he react when struck in the face by Yugloslav forward Jerkovic. USSR eventually won 2–0, but by then the game was totally out of control. Unsurprisingly, it was the first and last World Cup game refereed by Herr Dusch.

GRATEFUL PELÉ

The 1962 Group 3 match between Brazil and Czechoslovakia ended 0–0, and the closest the South Americans came to a goal was in the opening minutes when Pelé sliced through the defence and hit the post. In doing so, the 21-year-old genius aggravated a groin injury and was forced to spend the rest of the match lurking ineffectively on the wing. It was the end of his tournament, but the great man recalled later how Czech defenders Popluhar and Lala refused to go into any hard tackles whenever Pelé got the ball.

'It was one of those things I shall always remember with emotion, and one of the finest things that happened in my football career,' he said.

THE ATHLETE AND THE WORLD

It's only 36cm (14in) high, but it is the most famous sporting trophy of all. The World Cup is made of solid 18-carat gold and weighs 4,970 grams (11lb). Two rings of semi-precious malachite stones adorn the base. It was designed by Italian sculptor Silvio Gazzaniga in 1971, following a FIFA competition to design the cup after the Pelé-inspired Brazilians of 1970 took possession of the Jules Rimet Trophy with their third World Cup triumph, a 4–1 victory over Italy in Mexico. 'My inspiration for the design came from two basic elements – the athlete and the world,' Gazzaniga said. 'I had it in my mind to create something that symbolised effort and exertion, while at the same time expressing harmony, simplicity and peace.' He came up with two celebrating athletes, apparently lifting the world itself in a moment of sublime triumph.

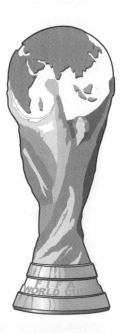

For FIFA, led by its English president Sir Stanley Rous, it was no contest, and Gazzaniga beat 52 other designs to win the commission.

THANKS, LADS!

The vituperative Italian press have always been quick to attack their own players, and often with good cause. But in 1962 Giovanni Ferrari's men had good reason to feel aggrieved over their coverage. Shortly before the tournament, two Italian journalists had published an excoriating attack on the host nation Chile, emphasising the poverty of Santiago, the corruption of the government and the dubious nocturnal activities of the local women. Not surprisingly, the Italian football team was greeted with a torrent of abuse whenever it took the field during the tournament, not least during the match against Chile when they were kicked and spat at. The Italians were knocked out in the first round and were no doubt relieved – until they returned home to find themselves lambasted by the Italian media for not performing.

THE EMPEROR'S NEW CLOTHES

Franz Beckenbauer was a footballing legend who had made 103 appearances for West Germany, played in three World Cups, two finals and lifted the trophy in 1974. Even so, there were those within the German game who had their doubts when he was made national team coach in 1984. For a start, he had no coaching licence. And, traditionally, the German boss was always succeeded by his qualified assistant. They needn't have worried: in 1986 Beckenbauer took his unfancied team to within an ace of beating Argentina in the final, and four years later in Italy became the second man, after Mario Zagallo, to win the World Cup both as a player and a coach. Der Kaiser indeed.

URUGUAY UNINSPIRING

Uruguay reached the second round of the 1986 World Cup without winning a game, scoring only one goal and having two players sent off.

LINEKER HAT TRICK

Gary Lineker's three goals against Poland in 1986 made him only the second England player to bag a World Cup hat trick. The first was Geoff Hurst twenty years earlier.

FRANCE AT LAST

When France beat Italy 2–0 in the second round of the 1986 tournament in Mexico, it was the first time they had beaten their European rivals in a major tournament since 1920.

BRAZIL OUT

Brazil crashed out of World Cup '86 after a quarter-final penalty shoot-out against France, and were understandably bemused to be flying home having won four, lost none, scored ten and conceded only one goal in the tournament.

FLARE-UP

The World Cup qualifier between Brazil and Chile in 1989 was an explosive match in more ways than one. Played in front of 114,000 screaming fans in Rio, Brazil were leading 1–0 and seemingly cruising to the finals in Italy when, after 69 minutes, a flare was thrown into the Chilean goalmouth. Roberto Rojas, the goalkeeper, fell writhing to the ground, apparently in agony after being struck on the head. The Chilean players refused to continue, claiming that the incident had left them physically and mentally shattered, and the game was abandoned. However, subsequent video footage revealed that the flare had missed Rojas by a mile and that his play-acting was just a cynical ploy to get the Brazilians disqualified. As a result Rojas was banned for life, as were the Chilean officials and medical staff who had happily joined in the con. The match was awarded 2–0 to Brazil, meaning Chile failed to qualify, and they were banned from the 1994 tournament for good measure.

TASTE OF SUCCESS

The first goal of the 1994 World Cup qualifying campaign was scored on 21 March 1992 by Mark Lugris, a New York restaurant manager, for Puerto Rico against the Dominican Republic.

ZAMBIA TRAGEDY

Zambia were one of the emerging powers in African football and firmly expected to do well in the 1994 World Cup finals in America. But, en route from Mauritius to Senegal to compete in a qualifying match on 27 April 1993, the military aircraft in which they were travelling crashed into the ocean off Gabon. Eighteen of the country's top players were killed. The tragedy united the nation and they resolved to continue their qualification bid. Needing just a draw against Morocco to reach the finals, Zambia were beaten 1–0.

HOME FLOPS

In 1994 none of the four home nation countries qualified for the World Cup finals, the first time this had happened since they had become eligible to compete. Both Andy Roxburgh of Scotland and Graham Taylor of England resigned as national managers after the failure.

WITCH DOCTOR

In an effort to qualify for the 1994 finals in the USA, Zimbabwe employed the services of a witch doctor before their vital match against Cameroon. Zimbabwe lost 3–1.

THE WRITE STUFF

Joao Saldanha, a Brazilian journalist, was such a vehement critic of the national side in the aftermath of the 1966 World Cup debacle that the Brazilian FA made the extraordinary decision to call his bluff and make him manager for the 1970 campaign. Unfortunately, Saldanha was better at dishing out criticism than he was at taking it and, after he was arrested at the house of a rival journalist brandishing a revolver, he was swiftly replaced in time for the 1970 tournament by Mario Zagallo, who had been a player in the 1958 and 1962 finals.

SUB SCORES

Juan Ignacio Basaguren's 83rd-minute goal for Mexico in their 4–0 win over El Salvador in 1970 made him the first substitute to score in a World Cup tournament. He had been on the pitch for just eight minutes.

HIGH FLYERS

The Group 2 game between Italy and Sweden in 1970 was played at the Luis Gutierrez Dosal stadium in Toluca, Mexico. At 8,744ft (2,665m) above sea-level it remains the highest World Cup match ever played.

CALAMITY JAMES

If, as the late Brian Clough insisted, it only takes a second to score a goal, then just think what can happen in two minutes. That's how long it took for England goalkeeper David James's world to collapse and for England's 2004 World Cup qualifier against Austria to turn to clay. With 71 minutes gone, Sven's men were leading 2–0 and playing comfortably for the win in Vienna. Then, against the run of play, substitute Ronald Kollmann bent home a free kick past the stranded James. It was a blow, though not the end of the world – but the goal gave the Austrians renewed confidence and for the next two minutes they launched an assault on the wobbly-looking England defence. Disaster almost inevitably struck: Andreas Ivanschitz struck a speculative-looking shot from the edge of the box which slithered under James's body into the net. England managed to hold on for the draw, but James's days as England's number one keeper were numbered – and what chances he had of being recalled were all but dashed eleven months later when, coming on as substitute during a friendly match against Denmark, he let in four second-half goals and claimed that he hadn't warmed up properly.

LIECHTENSTEIN ON A ROLL

It is highly unlikely that Liechtenstein will ever compete in the finals of a
World Cup. The tiny principality has a population of just 33,000 and its
football team consists of part-timers. Since they began entering World Cup
qualifiers in 1998, they have been beaten 11–1 by Macedonia and conceded
sixteen goals over two legs against Romania. In fact in 60 internationals,
Liechtenstein have only won once – against Azerbaijan. So it was
understandable that nobody in their right minds gave them a chance against
Portugal when the European Championship runners-up rolled into town for
a qualifying match in October 2004. For a while it was a sadly familiar story:
Pedro Pauleta scored after 23 minutes, and an own goal by Daniel Hasler
meant Liechtenstein were two goals down at half time. But whatever was said
during the interval clearly worked wonders. Three minutes into the second
half, Franz Burgmeier stunned the Portuguese with a crisp shot. But this was
nothing compared to the shock when Thomas Beck equalised after 76 minutes.
The draw earned Liechtenstein their first World Cup qualifying point after
twenty defeats in eight years, during which they had scored just four goals and
conceded 84. Astonishingly, they then went on to defeat Luxembourg 4–0 in
their next qualifying match to record their first win. Sadly, the team has since
lapsed into its losing ways once again.

THE RETURN OF SOCRATES

In his prime, Brasiliero Sampaio de Souza Vieira de Oliviera – aka Socrates –
was the fulcrum of the great Brazil team of 1982. When he retired after the
1986 finals, most people in Britain thought they'd seen the last of this brilliant,
elegant midfielder. In November 2004, however, he made a dramatic, not
to say astonishing, return – for Garforth Town, of the Northern Counties
East League Division One. Garforth's owner-manager Simon Clifford, a
successful businessman with contacts in Brazil, managed to persuade 50-year-
old Socrates (who was working as a doctor in Sao Paulo) to make a guest
appearance against Tadcaster. So it was that on a freezing cold day, with 78

minutes gone and the scores level at 2–2, the great man levered himself off the bench and trotted onto the pitch. In truth, the overweight and greying figure in the number six shirt was unrecognisable as the great player he had been in his slim-hipped prime, and it is estimated that he touched the ball no more than four times in his twelve-minute return to action. But those who were present will never forget the day a Brazilian legend played in the Northern Counties League.

DRUGGED?

In 1990 Brazil were beaten 1–0 by Argentina in a tense second-round knockout match in Turin. After the game, Brazil's Branco made the extraordinary claim that he had been drugged by a spiked water bottle handed to him by the Argentines. At the time the claim was dismissed as sour grapes – but then, in December 2004, Diego Maradona, who had been captain of the Argentina side that day, admitted that it was true and that the water bottle contained traces of the 'date-rape' drug Rohypnol. Although FIFA say they are powerless to act on the allegations, the incident has only increased the bitter rivalry between the two South American sides, and added an extra piquancy to all prospective World Cup encounters.

THE FINAL WORD

'There is too much bad behaviour in football now. Too much play acting and not enough respect for opponents and the referee. And the international players are treated like babies these days. Everything is done for them. We just had to muddle through on our own. And look what they are paid!'– Lucien Laurent, scorer of the first ever World Cup goal for France against Mexico on 13 July 1930. Lucien died in April 2005 aged 97.

ROBOCUP

Nobody knows who will contest the 2050 World Cup – or indeed whether it will be contested by humans at all. In 2003 a team of experts in the field of artificial intelligence announced they were embarking on a major project aimed at creating a team of 'fully autonomous humanoid robots' sufficiently skilled at football to be able to take on and beat the reigning human world champions by 2050.

ENGLAND'S WORLD CUP FINALS RECORD

- ⚽ **Most goals scored in a finals match** 4 (vs Belgium 1954, vs West Germany 1966)
- ⚽ **Largest margin of victory** 3 goals (vs Poland and Paraguay 1986, vs Denmark 2002)
- ⚽ **Largest margin of defeat** 2 goals (4–2 vs Uruguay 1954, 3–1 vs Brazil 1962)
- ⚽ **Number of scoreless draws** 8 (Brazil 1958, Bulgaria 1962, Uruguay 1966, West Germany and Spain 1982, Morocco 1986, Holland 1990, Nigeria 2002)
- ⚽ **Most matches in a tournament** 7 in 1990
- ⚽ **Fewest matches in a tournament** 3 in 1954 and 1958
- ⚽ **Most goals scored in a tournament** 11 in 1966
- ⚽ **Fewest goals scored in a tournament** 2 in 1950

SAD SEVENTIES

For a team which had been top of the world in the 1960s, the 1970s represented a period of unprecedented World Cup failure for England. The team which had been tipped to win the trophy in 1970 failed even to qualify for the finals under Alf Ramsey in 1974 and in 1978 under first Don Revie and then Ron Greenwood respectively. The full, dismal records make painful reading even now:

1974

Wales 0–1 England
England 1–1 Wales
Poland 2–0 England
England 1–1 Poland
(England finish second in the group and are eliminated)

1978

Finland 1–4 England
England 2–1 Finland
Italy 2–0 England
England 5–0 Luxembourg
Luxembourg 0–2 England
England 0–2 Italy
(England finish second in the group and are eliminated)

GREAT GAMES: Argentina 2–2 England
(4–3 after penalties), 1998
....

Perhaps not so great if you're an England supporter, but without doubt the best game of the 1998 tournament in France. Quite simply, the match had everything. And of course, it has the extra frisson of being between two old rivals who had never buried the hatchet since 1966. There were two spectacular goals by Owen and Zanetti, David Beckham's petulant kick at Simeone which earned him a red card, and then the agonies of yet another failed penalty shoot-out with David Batty's penalty being saved.

TRAVELLING WITH THE BARE MINIMUM

England named a 22-man squad for the 1954 tournament in Switzerland, but only seventeen players travelled to Switzerland. The other five squad members were left at home as reserves and were never called to active status. England named a 21-man squad for the 1950 tournament in Brazil, the lowest number they have ever called for a World Cup finals squad, but all players were members of the travelling party.

A LOAD OF BALLS

The first official World Cup ball was introduced in 1970 by Adidas, and was the now-classic 32-panel black-and-white Telstar ball. The different colours were aimed at making the ball more visible on black-and-white television sets. A similar Telstar ball was used for the 1974 finals. In 1978 the players used a Tango Durlast, and in 1982 the design was upgraded to make the ball waterproof. This was the last time a genuine leather football was used in the World Cup. The Azteca ball used in 1986 was coated in polyurethane, making it rain-resistant, and by 1994 the Questra ball featured an internal layer of polyurethane foam designed to improve control and also increase acceleration when it was kicked. In 1998 the first coloured ball was used, sporting the red, white and blue tricolour of France printed on an undercoat of syntactic foam. For the 2006 tourmament in Germany, Adidas produced the Teamgeist ball, made up of strange propeller-shaped panels 'designed to minimize corners and to create a more homogenous system in terms of performance and look'. The 2010 ball, unveiled in December 2009, was the Jabulani, which means 'to celebrate' or 'to bring joy' in isiZulu, one of the official languages of the host nation, South Africa. The aerodynamic design reflected the unique

African spirit and featured 11 different colours, representing the 11 players in a football team. The Brazuca, designed by Adidas for the 2014 World Cup, is said to be even more aerodynamic than its predecessor and features new panel shapes, a textured surface and a bold, colourful design.

ALL CHANGE FOR THE REFEREES

In 1930 the World Cup final between Uruguay and Argentina was refereed by John Langenus of Belgium, who wore a white dress shirt, dinner jacket, necktie and a pair of plus-fours, and who prepared for the big game by sitting down to a slap-up luncheon with other FIFA officials. It's a far cry from the gruelling preparation the referees for the 2006 World Cup finals were put through. At a special FIFA-organised workshop in February 2005 around 50 hopefuls were subjected to a thorough medical check-up and a number of theoretical and practical training sessions. They were also made to work on their physical fitness before being required to complete a demanding fitness test. For the rest of the year every one of their major matches was scrutinised by members of the FIFA refereeing panel and their performances assessed.

COSTA RICA RECORD

Costa Rica's shock 1–0 win over Scotland in their 1990 World Cup first match made them the first team from Central America ever to win a World Cup match in Europe.

BROTHERLY LOVE

In their 1990 first-round match against Colombia, the United Arab Emirates chose to field two sets of brothers: Eissa and Ibrahim Meer, and Nasser and Fahad Khamis.

OVERACTING

The Colombians have always flattered to deceive at World Cups, and 1990 in Italy was no exception. In fact, during their brief stay, the South Americans quickly became the team everybody loved to hate on account of their constant play-acting. The best moment came in their final group game against West Germany when skipper Carlos Valderrama went down under a non-existent challenge and lay there, writhing in pretend agony, for fully three minutes until he realised that the referee was having none of it. At which point he got up and continued playing.

PLAYING AWAY

Confined to the island of Sardinia for the duration of the first round of matches during Italia '90, England's players found different ways of relieving the boredom. Indeed Isabella Ciaravolo, their Sardinian liaison officer, was transferred elsewhere after unsubstantiated reports of her liaisons with members of the England squad!

CRUSHED

Tragedy marred the qualifying match between Guatemala and Costa Rica in 1993, when 60,000 people attempted to cram into a stadium with a capacity of just 45,000. In a hideous repeat of the Hillsborough disaster four years earlier, 84 people were asphyxiated against the perimeter fence in the resulting crush.

MONTEZUMA'S REVENGE?

Gordon Banks was undoubtedly the best goalkeeper in the world in 1970, as his save against Pelé in the Brazil match proved. But he was also only human – which was why his defences were powerless against an infamous dose of Montezuma's Revenge on the eve of the crunch match against West Germany in León. Alf Ramsey, paranoid about foreign food, had brought his own supplies with him. But Banks blamed his suffering on a 'dodgy bottle of Mexican beer'. And suffer he did. From both ends at the same time. Yet on the day of the match, Banks woke feeling much improved. Ramsey took a gamble and included him in the side. Then, shortly before kick-off, Banks suffered a relapse. As he retreated to his sickbed, the England boss informed reserve goalkeeper Peter Bonetti that he was in. Perhaps it was not the best preparation for the man known by Chelsea fans as 'The Cat': he was arguably at fault for all three German goals as England squandered a 2–0 lead to be eliminated from the tournament.

A VOTE OF NO CONFIDENCE

Midway through a 1993 qualifier against Iraq, Saudi Arabia's goalkeeper allowed the ball to trickle through his legs into the net. A watching Royal Prince immediately sent instructions to Saudi Arabia's Brazilian-born coach José Cândido to substitute the keeper. When he did not, Candido was sacked.

BOMB THREAT

Colombia started their 1994 World Cup pool game against the hosts USA without Gabriel Gomes after an unknown terrorist group threatened to blow his family up if he played. Those who thought this was an overreaction were given a salutary lesson in Colombian lawlessness when Andres Escobar – who had the misfortune to score an own goal in the match – was shot dead in Medellin just nine days later.

EARLY BATH FOR SONG

Cameroon's seventeen-year-old defender Rigobert Song became the youngest player to be sent off in a World Cup finals match when he was dismissed after 64 minutes of their group game against Brazil in 1994. He was red-carded again four years later against Chile.

OPRAH TAKES A TRIP AND MISS ROSS MISSES

The inaugural game in group C of the 1994 World Cup finals was played at Soldier Field in Chicago, and the organisers in the Windy City decided to pull out all the stops by inviting Diana Ross and chat-show queen Oprah Winfrey to appear in the grand opening ceremony. Sadly, things did not go to plan. First Oprah tripped up and went sprawling face first onto the stage. Then, just a few yards out and with an oversized net gaping, Ross somehow contrived to blast the ball wide from a staged penalty. This pre-match entertainment proved far more engaging than the match that followed, with Germany beating Bolivia by a single goal to nil.

ADIOS ETCHEVERRY

With ten minutes to go and trailing 1–0 to Germany in their opening pool match of the 1994 World Cup, Bolivia sent on star player Marco Etcheverry for his first game in over eight months following a serious knee injury. Two minutes later, Etcheverry was back in the dug-out having been sent off. He was banned from the next two matches, which effectively meant his World Cup was over.

BUNKING OFF

At fifteen years, four months and 28 days, Farooq Aziz became the youngest World Cup qualifier player when he appeared for Pakistan in an Asian group qualifier against China in 1993. In order to play, Farooq had first to get permission from his headmaster to take the afternoon off. Pakistan lost 5–0. However, the record was smashed in 2001 when Souleymane Mamam appeared as a substitute for Togo in a qualifying match against Zambia aged 13 years and 310 days old.

OLD QUALIFIER

Taylor MacDonald of the US Virgin Islands was 46 years and 180 days old
when he played against St Kitts & Nevis on 18 February 2004, making him the
oldest player ever to appear in a World Cup qualifier.

RAPID-FIRE SCORING

Abdelhamid Basuoni holds the record for the fastest World Cup hat trick
outside of the finals when he scored three times in just 177 seconds for Egypt
in a qualifier against Namibia in July 2002.

LITTLE EEL

Diego Maradona's brilliant second goal against England in the 1986 quarter-
final left most people speechless – but not Radio 2 commentator Bryon Butler,
whose now-classic description of the goal captured it perfectly:

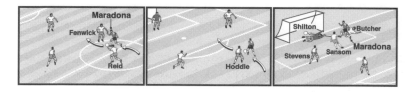

'Maradona turns like a little eel and comes away from trouble … Little squat
man … outside Fenwick, leaves him for dead … comes inside Terry Butcher,
leaves him for dead … And puts the ball away! … And that is why Maradona is
the greatest player in the world!'

TIGHT-KNIT SQUAD

When Brazil won the World Cup in 1962 they did so using just twelve players during the six-match tournament in Chile.

HOST OF GOOD FORTUNE

It certainly pays to host a World Cup finals. Since 1930 no host nation has failed to qualify from the first round, and only the USA (1994) and Japan (2002) did not reach the quarter-finals. Of the seventeen tournaments, six have been won by the host nation.

HITTING THE RIGHT NOTE

The closing ceremony of the 1990 World Cup in Rome was marked by a 'Century Gala' with a performance by the three tenors, Luciano Pavarotti, Plácido Domingo and José Carreras, who are avid soccer fans. It attracted a live audience of 6,000 and 1.5 billion TV viewers worldwide.

SMALL FRY

Berne, Switzerland, became the smallest city to host a World Cup final when Hungary and West Germany met each other in front of 62,000 spectators at the Wankdorf Stadium in 1954.

USA GETS THE BUG

Despite reputedly being a non-soccer country, USA '94 saw the highest total and average attendances in World Cup history. Some 3.5 million watched the matches at an average of 69,000 per game, compared with 2.5 million and 48,000 in football-mad Italy in 1990.

TRIBUTE TO AYRTON

The Brazil team dedicated their World Cup win in 1994 to the memory of racing driver and fellow countryman Ayrton Senna, who had been killed earlier that year in a horrific car crash at the Imola circuit in Italy.

LOW SCORE

The 1990 finals in Italy produced the lowest goals-per-game average of any World Cup – just 2.21. It also produced sixteen red cards and 164 yellows at an average of 3.46 cards per match, another unwelcome record.

LAST AND FIRST

Alessandro Altobelli of Italy scored the last goal of the 1982 tournament to secure a 3–1 win in the final against West Germany. He also scored the first goal of the 1986 finals, as the defending champions drew 1–1 with Bulgaria.

HELLO AND GOODBYE

Argentina's Marcelo Trobbiani made his one and only World Cup appearance as an 88th-minute substitute in the final against West Germany in 1986, equalling the record for the shortest World Cup career set by Tunisia's Khemais Labidi.

GOAL DIFFERENCE

The 1962 tournament in Chile was the first to apply the goal-difference ruling which would count in the event of two teams being equal on points in the first-round games. In the event, only England needed the new system to progress to the quarter-finals at the expense of Argentina.

VENUES

The stadiums selected as venues for the 1966 World Cup in England were:

- ⚽ Manchester (Old Trafford)
- ⚽ Middlesbrough (Ayresome Park)
- ⚽ Sunderland (Roker Park)
- ⚽ Liverpool (Goodison Park)
- ⚽ Sheffield (Hillsborough)
- ⚽ Birmingham (Villa Park)
- ⚽ London (Wembley, White City)

ENGLAND'S 1966 WORLD CUP-WINNING SQUAD

Goalkeepers Gordon Banks, Peter Bonetti, Ron Springett
Defenders Jimmy Armfield, Gerald Byrne, Jack Charlton, George Cohen, Bobby Moore (c), Ray Wilson
Midfielders Alan Ball, Ian Callaghan, Bobby Charlton, George Eastham, Ron Flowers, Norman Hunter, Martin Peters, Nobby Stiles
Forwards John Connelly, Jimmy Greaves, Roger Hunt, Geoff Hurst, Terry Paine
Coach Alf Ramsey

BROKEN LEG TRAGEDY

The USSR, winner of the inaugural European Nations Cup in 1960, beat Yugoslavia in their first World Cup match in 1962. But what should have been a day of triumph was spoiled when their right-back, Eduard Dubinsky, had his leg badly broken during the match in a vicious tackle by Yugoslav captain Muhamed Mujic. Dubinsky was hospitalised and his career was over, and then tragically the injury later caused sarcoma, a form of cancer, which claimed the player's life just a few years later.

A CUP WITHOUT JULES

The 1958 World Cup was the first to take place without the familiar figure of the competition's founder, Jules Rimet, who died two years earlier at the age of 83. He had been president of FIFA for a record 33 years.

MEMORABLE MORTENSEN

After boycotting the first three tournaments, England scored their first World Cup goal in the 39th minute of their opening match against Chile at the Maracana Stadium in Rio. The scorer was Stan Mortensen, who latched onto a cross by Jimmy Mullen to head the ball past the curiously named Sergio Livingstone in the Chilean goal.

BRAZIL NUTS ABOUT THE WORLD CUP

Thanks largely to the huge crowds, often in excess of 100,000, that packed into the vast bowl of the Maracana Stadium in Rio, the 1950 tournament in Brazil became the first major sporting event to be watched by more than a million spectators.

OUT AND ABOUT IN ITALY

Unlike the 1930 World Cup in Uruguay, when all games were played in Montevideo, eight venues were used in Italy four years later: Rome, Naples, Milan, Turin, Florence, Bologna, Genoa and Trieste.

CURING THE HOMER SYMPTOM

Until Spain's victory in South Africa in 2010, no European team had ever won the World Cup outside their home continent.

GREAT GAMES: Romania 3–2 Argentina, 1994

....

Despite losing Maradona to a FIFA ban for drug-taking, Argentina were no pushovers. But then neither were Romania, whose collective will to win, allied to the clever prompting of Hagi and Dumitrescu, made them the dark horses of the tournament. And despite the best efforts of the reigning World Champions, Romania came good in a fantastic match of swinging fortunes, close shaves and spectacular goals.

WHERE THE FINALS WERE PLAYED

Year	Country	City	Stadium	Attendance
1930	Uruguay	Montevideo	Estadio Centenario	93,000
1934	Italy	Rome	Stadio Nazionale	50,000
1938	France	Paris	Stade Colombes	45,124
1950	Brazil	Rio	Maracana	205,000
1954	Switzerland	Berne	Wankdorf Stadium	62,472
1958	Sweden	Stockholm	Rasunda Stadium	49,737
1962	Chile	Santiago	Estadio Nacional	68,679
1966	England	London	Wembley Stadium	93,802
1970	Mexico	Mexico City	Azteca Stadium	107,412
1974	West Germany	Munich	Olympic Stadium	77,833
1978	Argentina	Buenos Aires	Monumental Stadium	76,609
1982	Spain	Madrid	Bernabeu Stadium	90,089
1986	Mexico	Mexico City	Azteca Stadium	114,580
1990	Italy	Rome	Olympic Stadium	73,603
1994	USA	Pasadena	Rose Bowl	94,194
1998	France	Paris	Stade de France	75,000
2002	Japan/S. Korea	Yokohama	Yokohama International	69,029
2006	Germany	Berlin	Olympiastadion	69,000
2010	South Africa	Johannesburg	Soccer City	84,490

FOREIGN FOOD

On their way to the 1962 World Cup semi-final, the Chilean team claimed their diet was the major reason for success. No doubt in a very early version of media spin, they claimed they ate Swiss cheese to beat the Swiss and spaghetti to beat Italy, and drank vodka to beat the USSR. Brazilian coffee clearly didn't agree with them, because they were beaten 4–2 by Garrincha and co.

A FIRST FOR BERLIN

The Olympic Stadium in Berlin hosted the 2006 World Cup final. But although the design was all-new, the stadium has a long and chequered history. Here are ten things you should know:

⚽ The original stadium was built to house the aborted 1916 Olympics.
⚽ The stadium was rebuilt by Hitler for the 1936 Olympics. After the war, it was used by the British army as their headquarters and remained so until 1994.
⚽ The 1936 stadium was built by the son of the architect who designed the 1916 version.
⚽ The stadium is the home ground of Hertha Berlin.
⚽ It was used for three matches in the 1974 World Cup finals.
⚽ The stadium was renovated in 2004 after Germany was given the go-ahead to host the 2006 finals.
⚽ It hosted six matches in 2006, including the final.
⚽ The capacity is 76,000, making it the second largest stadium in Germany behind the Olympic Stadium in Munich.
⚽ It cost €240 million (£140 million) to renovate.
⚽ The roof on the stands is a cantilever with a circumference of 840m (2756ft).

HOME FROM HOME

At the 1950 World Cup, Chile's George Robledo was the only English-based player (outside the England team, naturally), plying his trade with Newcastle

United. Today almost two thirds of the English Premier League is made up of foreign players, and many familiar names will be included in World Cup squads heading for Brazil this summer. The foreign legion could include:

ALGERIA Adlène Guedioura (Crystal Palace)
ARGENTINA Fabricio Coloccini, Jonas Gutierrez (Norwich City, on loan from Newcastle United), Sergio Aguero, Martin Demichelis, Pablo Zabaleta (Manchester City), Luciano Becchio (Norwich), Paulo Gazzaniga (Southampton), Julian Speroni (Crystal Palace), Erik Lamela (Tottenham Hotspur), Claudio Yacob (West Bromwich Albion)
AUSTRALIA Chris Herd (Aston Villa), Mile Jedinak (Crystal Palace), Brad Jones (Liverpool), Mark Schwarzer (Chelsea)
BELGIUM Christian Benteke (Aston Villa), Nacer Chadli, Mousa Dembele, Jan Vertonghen (Tottenham), Eden Hazard (Chelsea), Marouane Fellaini, Adnan Januzaj (Manchester United), Vincent Kompany (Manchester City), Kevin Mirallas, Romelu Lukaku (Everton, on loan from Chelsea), Simon Mignolet (Liverpool), Thomas Vermaelen (Arsenal)
BOSNIA-HERZEGOVINA Asmir Begovic (Stoke City), Edin Dzeko (Manchester City)
BRAZIL Rafael da Silva (Manchester United), Philippe Coutinho, Lucas Leiva (Liverpool), David Luiz, Oscar, Ramires, Willian (Chelsea), Guly do Prado (Southampton), Fernandinho (Manchester City), Heurelmo Gomes, Paulinho, Sandro (Tottenham)
CAMEROON Benoit Assou-Ekotto (QPR, on loan from Tottenham), Sebastian Bassong (Norwich City), Samuel Eto'o (Chelsea)
CHILE Gary Medel (Cardiff City)
COLOMBIA Hugo Rodallega (Fulham)
CROATIA Nikica Jelavic (Hull City), Dejan Lovren (Southampton)
ECUADOR Antonio Valencia (Manchester United)
FRANCE Nicolas Anelka (West Bromwich Albion), Nabil Bentaleb, Etienne Capoue, Younes Kaboul, Hugo Lloris (Tottenham), Hatem Ben Arfa, Yohan Cabaye, Mathieu Debuchy, Yoan Gouffran, Massadio Haidara, Sylvain

Marveaux, Gabriel Obertan, Moussa Sissoko, Mapuo Yanga-Mbiwa (Newcastle United), Mamadou Sakho (Liverpool), Abou Diaby, Mathieu Flamini, Olivier Giroud, Laurent Koscielny, Bacary Sagna, Yaya Sanogo (Arsenal), Modibo Diakite, Valentin Roberge (Sunderland), Alou Diarra (West Ham), Sylvain Distin (Everton), Patrice Evra (Manchester United), Gael Clichy, Samir Nasri (Manchester City), Charles N'Zogbia (Aston Villa), Steven N'Zonz (Stoke City), Morgan Schneiderlin (Southampton), Loïc Rémy (QPR, on loan from Newcastle United).

GERMANY Nick Proschwitz (Hull City), Serge Gnabry, Per Mertesacker, Mesut Ozil, Lukas Podolski (Arsenal), Robert Huth (Stoke City), Andre Schurrle (Chelsea), Sascha Riether (Fulham), Gerhard Tremmel (Swansea City)

GHANA Derek Boateng (Fulham), Michael Essien (Chelsea), Emmanuel Frimpong (Arsenal)

GREECE Giorgos Karagounis (Fulham), Charalampos Mavrias (Sunderland), Apostolos Vellios (Everton)

HOLLAND Vurnon Anita, Tim Krul (Newcastle United), Leandro Bacuna, Ron Vlaar (Aston Villa), Alexander Buttner, Robin van Persie (Manchester United), Marco van Ginkel (Chelsea), Jonathan de Guzman, Michel Vorm (Swansea), John Heitinga (Everton), Erik Pieters (Stoke City), Maarten Stekelenberg (Fulham), Ricky van Wolfswinkel (Norwich City)

HONDURAS Maynor Figueroa (Hull City), Wilson Palacios (Stoke City)

IRAN Ashkan Dejagah (Fulham)

ITALY Fabio Borini (Sunderland, on loan from Liverpool), Andrea Dossena, Emanuele Giaccherini, Vito Mannone (Sunderland), Federico Macheda (Manchester United), Pablo Osvaldo (Southampton), Davide Santon (Newcastle United)

IVORY COAST Wilfried Bony (Swansea), Arouna Kone (Everton), Yaya Toure (Manchester City), Yannick Sagbo (Hull City), Cheick Tiote (Newcastle United), Kolo Toure (Liverpool)

JAPAN Shinji Kagawa (Manchester United), Maya Yoshida (Southampton), Ryo Miyaichi (Arsenal)

MEXICO Javier Hernandez (Manchester United)

NIGERIA Shola Ameobi (Newcastle United), Victor Anichebe (West Bromwich Albion), Sone Aluko (Hull City), John Obi Mikel (Chelsea), Victor Moses (Liverpool), Peter Odemwingie (Cardiff City)
PORTUGAL José Fonte (Southampton), Nani (Manchester United), Ricardo Vaz Te (West Ham United)
SOUTH KOREA Ki Sung-Yueng (Sunderland, on loan from Swansea), Kim Bo-Kyung (Cardiff City), Park Chu-Young (Arsenal)
SPAIN Mikel Arteta, Santi Cazorla, Nacho Monreal (Arsenal), Javier Garrido (Norwich City), Cesar Azpilicueta, Fernando Torres (Chelsea), José Campana (Crystal Palace), José Canas, Chico Flores, Pablo Hernandez, Michu, Alejandro Pozuelo, Angel Rangel (Swansea), Carlos Cuellar (Sunderland), David de Gea, Juan Mata (Manchester United), José Enrique (Liverpool), Antonio Luna (Aston Villa), Jesus Navas, Alvaro Negredo, David Silva (Manchester City), Roberto Soldado (Tottenham)
SWITZERLAND Pajtim Kasami, Philippe Senderos (Fulham)
UNITED STATES Jozy Altidore (Sunderland), Geoff Cameron (Stoke City), Clint Dempsey (Fulham, on loan from Seattle Sounders), Maurice Edu (Stoke City), Brad Friedel (Tottenham), Brad Guzan (Aston Villa), Tim Howard (Everton)
URUGUAY Luis Suarez (Liverpool), Gaston Ramirez (Southampton)

HOW IT ALL BEGAN

International football had been around since the late 19th century, and by 1908 the Olympic Games had its own fully fledged tournament (the UK beat Denmark to win gold). By the late 1920s, however, the growth of the game – and in particular professionalism – meant that football was crying out for a competition of its own. FIFA (Fédération Internationale de Football Association) had been formed in 1904 and in 1929, 25 of its 30 member nations voted for a tournament to be held within a year. The architects of the first World Cup were French. The original idea was drafted by FIFA member Henry Delaunay and the final nod of assent to the tournament was given by the president of the organisation, Jules Rimet. If they'd had it their way, the first tournament would have been held in France too – but there was only one member nation willing not only to meet the costs of staging such a global event but to pay the expenses of every country that took part. So it was that in 1930 the first World Cup took place in Uruguay.

GOLDEN BALLS

Since 1982 the most outstanding player of the tournament has received the Golden Ball. The winner is voted for by the media from a shortlist drawn up by the FIFA technical committee. The second and third-placed runners-up in this vote are awarded the silver ball and the bronze ball:

1982 SPAIN

1. Paolo Rossi (ITA) Goals 6, assists 0, mins played 575
2. Falcao (BRA) Goals 3, assists 0, mins played 450
3. Karl-Heinz Rummenigge (GER) Goals 5, assists 0, mins played 572

1986 MEXICO

1. Diego Maradona (ARG) Goals 5, assists 0, mins played 572
No silver or bronze balls were officially awarded in 1986, although they were retrospectively awarded to Harald Schumacher (GER) and Preben Elkjær (DEN).

1990 ITALY

1. Salvatore Schillaci (Italy) Goals 6, assists 0, mins played 535
2. Lothar Matthaus (GER) Goals 4, assists 0, mins played 660
3. Diego Maradona (ARG) Goals 0, assists 0, mins played 690

1994 USA

1. Romario (BRA) Goals 5, assists 0, mins played 660
2. Roberto Baggio (ITA) Goals 5, assists 0, mins played 603
3. Hristo Stoichkov (BUL) Goals 6, assists 0, mins played 644

1998 FRANCE
1. Ronaldo (BRA) Goals 5, assists 0, mins played 660
2. Davor Suker (CRO) Goals 6, assists 0, mins played 630
3. Lilian Thuram (FRA) Goals 2, assists 0, mins played 600

2002 KOREA/JAPAN
1. Oliver Kahn (GER) Goals 0, assists 0 (GK), mins played 630
2. Ronaldo (BRA) Goals 8, assists 0, mins played 548
3. Hong Myung Bo (KOR) Goals 0, assists 0, mins played 596

2006 GERMANY
1. Zinedine Zidane (FRA) Goals 3, assists 1, mins played 559
2. Fabio Cannavaro (ITA) Goals 0, assists 0, mins played 690
3. Andrea Pirlo (ITA) Goals 1, assists 3, mins played 668

2010 SOUTH AFRICA
1. Diego Forlan (URU) Goals 5, assists 1, mins played 564
2. Wesley Sneijder (HOL) Goals 5, assists 1, mins played 653
3. David Villa (SPA) Goals 5, assists 1, mins played 635

OH NO, GINOLA

Despite possessing one of the most talented squads in the world, France failed to make the 1994 finals in the USA. The manner of their elimination was painful to behold – and especially for one of the most talented Frenchmen of them all. With the score at 1–1 and needing only to draw against Bulgaria to secure qualification after a ropey passage which had included defeat to Israel, the French were awarded a free kick deep in opposition territory. There were just 30 seconds of time remaining and already 70,000 fans in the Parc des Princes were thinking about buying plane tickets to the States. Then, disaster. The ball found David Ginola, the long-haired, extravagantly talented left-winger. Instead of playing keep-ball for the remaining seconds, Ginola instead took on his man and lofted a curling cross into the box. The French forwards were not expecting it, and neither were the rest of the team as Bulgaria nabbed possession and broke forward with lightning speed. The ball found Emil Kostadinov, who thrashed it into the back of the net with just ten seconds remaining. France were out of the World Cup and despite his grovelling apology – 'I have no words to describe this moment' – Ginola would never play for his country again.

MARADONA'S FALL FROM GRACE

After lighting up the 1986 and, to a lesser extent the 1990, tournaments, Diego Maradona was hauled back from retirement to bolster a struggling Argentina side in their 1994 campaign in the USA. Despite four turbulent years of cocaine abuse during which he had attacked reporters with an air rifle, Maradona arrived in the US looking leaner and fitter than ever before and it seemed at first that the little man's presence was indeed having a galvanising effect on his teammates. In their first game against Greece, Argentina were ahead after just 70 seconds and went on to canter home 4–0. Maradona himself scored a wondrous third goal, but this was overshadowed by an extraordinary celebration in which his wide-eyed mask of triumph was thrust directly into the lens of a pitch-side camera. It was not until after the next game, a 2–1 win over Nigeria, that his behaviour was explained. A drugs test revealed a cocktail of five banned drugs in his bloodstream, all belonging to the ephedrine family. Ephedrine, while most commonly found in nasal sprays, is also a stimulant which can aid weight loss. Despite the usual pleas of ignorance, the greatest player of modern times was caught red-handed and immediately kicked out of the tournament and banned from the game. He returned to Argentina in disgrace – ironically needing to have played just one more game to break the record for World Cup appearances.

JACK'S BOYS DO THE BUSINESS

When Ireland played their opening match of the 1994 World Cup at the Giants Stadium in New York, it is estimated that more than 50,000 of the 73,000 capacity crowd were supporting Jack Charlton's men as they defeated Italy 1–0.

GORDON BANKS'S SAVE

In an earlier game against Czechoslovakia in 1970, Pelé had come within inches of scoring a sensational goal when his 60-yard shot just missed the post. Against England, the Brazilian wizard was responsible for forcing what is widely regarded as the competition's most extraordinary save when his bullet header was somehow clawed off the line and over the bar by Gordon Banks. What made the save special was that in order to make it, Banks had to leap from his near post to the far post in a split-second, twisting in mid-air in order to get his outstretched hand to the ball.

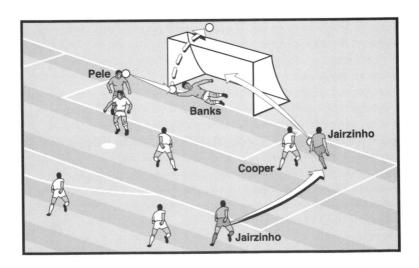

SENT-OFF KEEPER

Although the dubious honour should have, without doubt, gone to West Germany's Harald Schumacher for his assault on Battiston twelve years earlier, the first goalkeeper to be sent off in World Cup finals was Italy's Gianluca Pagliuca for the comparatively mild offence of handling the ball outside his penalty area during a match against Norway in 1994.

EURO QUARTERS

In 1994 all but one of the quarter-finalists were from Europe, the first time since 1958. In both cases the sole South American representative was Brazil — and on both occasions they went on to lift the trophy.

LANGUAGE BARRIER

Cameroon were the surprise performers of the 1990 World Cup, beating Argentina, Colombia and Romania before almost defeating England in the quarter-finals. What made their progress even more remarkable was that they were coached by Valeri Nepomniaschi, a Siberian whose only previous managerial experience was in the Soviet second division. Because he spoke no French, Nepomniaschi relied upon a driver from the Soviet embassy in Rome to translate his team talks — and it was widely suspected that the driver, himself a keen amateur player, infused many of the manager's tactics with his own.

THE HAND OF GOD — AGAIN

Maradona's personal relationship with the Hand of God made headlines in 1986, and four years later in Italy it seemed the bond was just as strong. Under the cosh against the Soviet Union in their pool match in Bari, the Argentine skipper found himself defending his own goal-line as a header from Kuznetzov arrowed its way towards the net. It would have been a certain goal had the Hand of God not shot out to deflect the ball round the post. In many ways Maradona's handball was even more blatant than the one against England – but, miraculously, referee Erik Frederiksson of Sweden didn't see it. Argentina went on to win 2–0, Maradona went unpunished, and the only sinner was deemed to be Frederiksson who was sent home early, accused of incompetence.

DON'T COUNT OUT COSTA RICA

During the course of their 1990 qualifying campaign, Costa Rica went through five managers and three FA presidents. It was no surprise, then, that the minnows were rated at a whopping 1,000–1 outsiders to win in Italy. Even less of a surprise was that in their first game they beat Scotland by a goal to nil. Managed by Velibor Milutinovic, who had been in charge of hosts Mexico in 1986, they would confound everyone by also beating Sweden and qualifying for the next phase.

STATUESQUE GOALKEEPER

Undisputed hero of Costa Rica's epic 1990 World Cup run was goalkeeper Gabelo Conejo, whose acrobatics between the sticks helped propel the 1,000–1 outsiders to the second phase. After the tournament, a statue was erected in Conejo's honour in the Costa Rican capital San José.

STALLED FERRARI

As an incentive to qualify for the second phase of the 1990 World Cup, each United Arab Emirates player was promised the reward of a Ferrari Testarossa. Sadly they lost all three pool games, conceding eleven goals. However, striker Khalid Mubarak did bag himself a Rolls-Royce for scoring the UAE's only goal. In 1994 each member of the team received £100,000 and a new Mercedes for qualifying for the finals.

MANAGEMENT MATERIAL?

In later years they would both become managers of their respective countries, but as players in 1990, Holland's Frank Rijkaard and Rudi Voller of West Germany provided one of the World Cup's more memorable spats – literally:

1. 21 minutes have been played. Rijkaard fouls Voller, who dives outrageously.
2. Referee Jana Carlos Loustau of Argentina cautions Rijkaard, which means he will be suspended for the next game.
3. Rijkaard spits at Voller, who complains to the referee.
4. The referee books Voller.
5. Two minutes later Voller and Rijkaard get tangled up in another challenge.
6. The referee sends both players off.
7. As they leave the pitch, Rijkaard spits at Voller one more time.

TOO MUCH TO BEAR

England squeaked past Cameroon to reach the semi-finals of the 1990 World Cup, but it was the Africans who had captured the hearts of the estimated two billion TV viewers watching the tournament across the world. Their departure was too much to bear for one Bangladeshi woman, however, who hanged herself shortly after the final whistle. Her suicide note read: 'The elimination of Cameroon also means the end of my life.'

NATIONAL FERVOUR

Before Argentina's 1990 quarter-final against Italy, Diego Maradona – then playing for Napoli – urged all Neapolitans to support the South American side, claiming that for centuries they had been oppressed by the rich north of the country. Needless to say, he was roundly booed from that moment on.

PENALTY

World Cup 1990 was the first time both semi-finals were decided by penalty shoot-outs.

NESSUN DORMA

Pavarotti's version of Nessun Dorma became a huge hit when it was used as the theme tune for BBC's coverage of the 1990 World Cup finals in Italy. The Beeb were about to commission their own music when presenter Desmond Lynam suggested the Puccini aria. Its success led to a resurgence in the popularity of opera, and in the career of Pavarotti, who subsequently joined forces to sing it with Plácido Domingo and José Carreras in their globetrotting Three Tenors tours.

GAZZA'S TEARS

Paul Gascoigne had been the undisputed star of England's rollercoaster World Cup '90, which began ignominiously but ended with Bobby Robson's men very nearly reaching the final. It was in the semi-final against West Germany that the bubbly Geordie – described by Robson as being 'daft as a brush' – captured the hearts of the world. With the scores tied and the match into extra time Gazza lunged at Berthold and was booked. The yellow card meant only one thing: if England won, Gascoigne would have to sit out the final. Gazza knew this all too well – and promptly burst into floods of tears. 'Have a word with him,' a concerned Gary Lineker mouthed to the touchline. To his credit, Gazza played on with his customary ebullience as England earned a penalty shoot-out. But although the Germans won through to the final, Gascoigne's global fame and subsequent riches meant that the match had only one winner.

ZENGA BEATEN

Claudio Caniggia's goal for Argentina in the 67th minute of their semi-final tie against Italy in 1990 was the first to be conceded by Italian goalkeeper Walter Zenga in 517 minutes of World Cup football. Zenga's record eclipsed that of England's Peter Shilton by just eighteen minutes but Italy were defeated in a penalty shoot-out.

BRAZIL CHEEK

Having won the World Cup in 1958 and 1962, Brazil were understandably favourites to complete their hat trick in England in 1966. Indeed the Brazilians were so confident of winning, and thereby keeping the Jules Rimet trophy in perpetuity, they even offered to replace it with another called the Winston Churchill Cup. In the end, they would have to wait four more years before claiming the Jules Rimet trophy as their own, winning the World Cup in Mexico in 1970.

BERT ON THE MARK

First player to score a hat trick in a World Cup match was Bert Patenaude of the USA, who bagged three against Paraguay in the first round of the 1930 World Cup in Uruguay.

LOTS

The Republic of Ireland and Holland finished with identical records in Group F of the 1990 World Cup finals in Italy, and with England winning the group, had to draw lots for second and third places. Ireland drew second and went on to face Romania; Holland played West Germany.

WORLD CUP ALL-TIME TOP SCORERS 1930–2013

15   Ronaldo (BRA)

14   Miroslav Klose (GER), Gerd Muller (GER)

13   Just Fontaine (FRA)

12   Pelé (BRA)

11   Jurgen Klinsmann (GER), Sandor Kocsis (HUN)

10   Gabriel Batistuta (ARG), Gary Lineker (ENG), Teofilo Cubillas (PER), Grzegorz Lato (POL), Helmut Rahn (GER)

9   Roberto Baggio (ITA), Paolo Rossi (ITA), Uwe Seeler (GER), Jairzinho (BRA), Eusebio (POR), Karl-Heinz Rummenigge (GER), Vava (BRA), Ademir (BRA), Christian Vieri (ITA)

8   Diego Maradona (ARG), David Villa (SPA), Guillermo Stabile (ARG), Leonidas (BRA), Rivaldo (BRA), Rudi Voller (GER), Oscar Miguez (URU)

SUKUR PUNCH

One of the biggest surprises about Vaclav Masek's goal for Czechoslovakia after just fifteen seconds of their tie against Mexico in 1962 is that it should stand for so long as the quickest in a World Cup. After all, fifteen seconds is quite a long time when, as Brian Clough once observed, it only takes a second to score a goal. In fact the record would last for 40 years. It was finally shattered by Turkey's Hakan Sukur in the third-place playoff match against co-hosts South Korea on 28 June 2002. Just eleven seconds were on the clock when Sukur pounced on a defensive error to hammer the ball into the back of the net.

SAND OF TIME

The fastest goal by a substitute was scored by Ebbe Sand of Denmark against Nigeria in the second round in 1998. Sand scored only sixteen seconds after coming on in Denmark's 4–1 win.

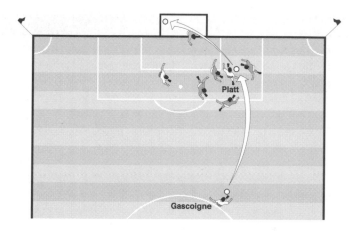

LAST-GASP PLATT

England's 1990 World Cup campaign is remembered fondly as the one that got away, thanks to West Germany's unerring accuracy in penalty shoot-outs. But the rose-tinted spectacles hide what was, for the most part, a finals to which Bobby Robson's men were clinging on by their fingernails. Having stuttered through the first round, their second-round match against Belgium was just a minute away from penalties when Gerets brought down Gascoigne 40 yards out. Gazza's precise, inswinging free kick was met by David Platt (a 71st minute substitute for Steve McMahon), who got his foot around the ball and diverted it into the net past Preud'homme. Timed at 119 minutes, it remains the latest goal ever scored in a World Cup tie.

OLD RIVALS

Sweden have played Brazil seven times in World Cup history. No other countries have met more often.

KISS OF DEATH

The fastest hat trick in World Cup history was scored by Hungary's Laszlo Kiss, who scored in the 70th, 74th and 77th minutes against El Salvador in 1982. The feat is somewhat diminished by the fact that the South Americans were already 5–1 down and would go on to lose the match by a record score of 10–1. But then again, Kiss had only been on the field himself for fifteen minutes, having come on as a second-half substitute (he is, in fact, the only substitute to have scored a hat trick).

THE ETERNAL NUMBER 12

Poland's Leslaw Cmikiewiez played in all six matches of Poland's 1974 World Cup campaign – coming on as substitute each time.

MILLA TIME

An indication of the longevity of Cameroon's Roger Milla is that his final appearance in a World Cup finals was in 1994 – eighteen years since he first won Africa's footballer of the year award at the age of 24. In the USA Milla was 42 years old and even he would admit he was past his sell-by date. Cameroon, similarly, were but a shadow of the team which had delighted the world by reaching the quarter-finals four years earlier. This time they failed to win a game. However this did not stop Milla appearing twice as a substitute and scoring his customary goal. In fact his close-range toe-poke against Russia in the 47th minute made him not only the oldest player to have scored a goal in a World Cup, but at the time the fastest substitute scorer, having been brought on at half time.

PELÉ STATES HIS CASE

There were those in the Brazilian camp who thought Pelé was too young and irresponsible to play for the team in the 1958 World Cup finals. They soon changed their minds when he produced a sublime performance in his debut in the second round against the USSR. And the youngster reinforced his point in the quarter-final match against Wales with a deflected goal in the 71st minute. Aged just seventeen years and 239 days, he remains the youngest player to have scored in a World Cup.

GOAL A GAME

The only players to have scored in every World Cup match are Alcide Ghiggia of Uruguay, who managed the feat in 1950, and Jairzinho of Brazil, who did it twenty years later. Of the two, Jairzinho's achievement is the more impressive, as he played in six games whereas Ghiggia scored in every match but Uruguay only played four games.

FOUR AN UNLUCKY NUMBER

On any other day, Polish marksman Ernst Willimowski's feat of scoring four goals in a World Cup match would have grabbed all the headlines and made him a global superstar. Sadly Willimowski's moment of glory came in 1938 against Brazil, who just happened to score six that day to secure a 6–5 victory. The four goals also lose lustre if you consider that Brazil's Leonidas is credited with scoring four himself that day (although some sources claim he only scored three). At least Willimowski earns himself the dubious accolade of being the only man in World Cup history to score four goals and end up on the losing side.

A GOAL FOR EACH SIDE

Robert Prosinecki is the only player in World Cup history to have scored for two countries. In 1990, representing Yugoslavia, he bagged a goal against the United Arab Emirates. Eight years later, Yugoslavia was no more and Prosinecki was playing for Croatia when he scored against Jamaica.

OH NO – OWN GOAL!

It's the record that nobody wants but somebody has to have – and the honour goes to the unfortunate Ernst Lotscher of Switzerland who in 1938 became the first player to score an own goal in a World Cup match when he put one through his own net in a first-round replay against Germany.

SUBS UP IN MEXICO

Up until 1970, the use of substitutes was seen as somewhat unmanly. Unless they had a broken leg, players even at the very top level tended to play on. The Mexico tournament, as well as being the first to introduce red and yellow cards, was also the first to feature substitutes. The first was Anatoly Puzach of the USSR, who came on at half time in the opening match against Mexico.

GREAT GAMES: Belgium 4–3 USSR (aet), 1986

In the sweltering heat of León in Mexico, few expected two European sides to produce such superb entertainment – but Belgium and the USSR conjured a seven-goal thriller in which the only unfortunate aspect was that one of them had to be eliminated from the tournament at the end. Belanov, European Footballer of the Year, started the ball rolling with a magnificent strike after 27 minutes – one of three goals for the Soviet star in the match. But in a game of roller-coaster fortunes, rattling woodwork, penalty appeals and two suspicious-looking Belgian goals, the match was decided in extra time with goals by Demol and Claesen.

THE HAND OF GOD

No matter how many brilliant goals Diego Maradona scored in his long World Cup career, the one which stands out more than any other – more even than the magnificent 50-yard solo dribble that followed it – is the so-called 'Hand of God' goal against England in the quarter-final of the 1986 tournament in Mexico. The facts of the matter are these: in the 51st minute Steve Hodge attempted a clearance from the edge of his own penalty area which sliced horrendously across the 18-yard line; Maradona raced in and jumped with Peter Shilton; Maradona punched the ball over Shilton's head into the back of the net; the referee allowed the goal. The Argentine skipper later described his deliberate handball as 'The Hand of God', and for some bizarre reason that excuse seemed to placate the authorities, who could have issued Maradona with a one-match ban. Instead, he was vindicated by his second goal four minutes later and by his all-round brilliance in the tournament as a whole. Would England have won if their confidence hadn't been rocked by Maradona's cheating? Probably not. After all, the West Germans failed to recover from Geoff Hurst's debatable second goal in the 1966 final. But in 1986 television technology was twenty years advanced, and it was clear from the very first replay that the goal should not have stood. Maradona and Argentina went on to win the match and the World Cup.

GOAL IN A THOUSAND

With Scotland needing to win by three clear goals against Holland to salvage their disastrous 1978 World Cup campaign, there was a great deal at stake when Stuart Kennedy upended Johnny Rep to concede a 34th minute penalty. Certainly no-one in the San Martin stadium in Mendoza was aware that if Robbie Rensenbrink converted the spot kick he would be reaching a World Cup milestone, least of all Rensenbrink himself. The Dutchman duly scored and thereby notched the 1,000th goal in World Cup history.

GOLDEN GOAL

Ever since it was invented, football mandarins have been trying to get rid of the dreaded penalty shoot-out as a means of deciding stalemate matches. In 1996 FIFA introduced the so-called 'Golden Goal' in the European

Championships in England. It meant that if a match went into extra time, the first team to score would immediately win the match. On paper it seemed like a good idea – but when a Golden Goal decided the final between Germany and the Czech Republic, fans were left feeling even more cheated than if the match had been decided on penalties. The system was used for the first time in the World Cup two years later, and, fittingly, it was France who benefited when Laurent Blanc's extra-time strike secured a 1–0 win over Paraguay. In 2003, the Golden Goal became the Silver Goal – this time the team leading after the first fifteen-minute period of extra time would win. Thankfully in 2004 the whole system was scrapped. It seemed that, however unsatisfactory, penalties were here to stay.

SWEATING IN MOTOWN

In a bid to add some razzmatazz to the 1994 World Cup, the Americans decreed that the match between the hosts and Switzerland would be played, for the first time, indoors. The venue was the Pontiac Silverdome in Detroit. Usually the home of the Detroit Lions grid-iron team, the stadium is perfect for those freezing Midwest nights during the NFL season. But in the height of a roasting summer, and with 73,000 fans packed to the rafters, the effect was to slowly boil the players of both sides and coat the grass with a veneer of moisture. It was not long before the teams were reduced to walking pace, and those who tried to run found themselves slipping on the greasy surface. The match finished 1–1, which in itself was an effort worthy of congratulation.

NORTH KOREA MAGIC

For the people of Middlesbrough, the North Korean side of 1966 must have seemed impossibly exotic – if not a little frightening. But it did not take long for the men from South East Asia to win the hearts of the Teessiders, with a series of tenacious displays culminating in one of the greatest upsets in World Cup history. Playing with plenty of enthusiasm but little guile, the North

Koreans were hammered 3–0 in their first match against the Soviet Union. In their next match, however, they gave an indication of things to come by playing out a spirited 1–1 draw with Chile. Their final group game was against the mighty Italians, who had struggled to beat Chile and gone down 1–0 to the Soviets. Nevertheless, they were expected to crush the North Koreans and thereby qualify for the next round. Fielding seven changes, Italy set about the minnows with gusto. But brave defending kept the scores level, and then things gradually began to fall apart for Fabri, the Italian manager. First Bulgarelli departed with a knee injury after 35 minutes. Then, with just three minutes to go to half time, a sweeping North Korean move ended with Pak Doo-ik scoring with a spectacular strike. Stunned, the Italians were unable to rouse themselves in the second half and, to the delight of the underdog-supporting Englishmen packed into Ayresome Park, North Korea ran out winners. Things got even worse for the Italians who, having been ignominiously eliminated, returned to a barrage of rotten fruit and vegetables at Rome airport.

NORTH KOREA AGAIN

Having stunned the footballing world by beating Italy in the group stages of the 1966 finals, North Korea seemed destined to create an even bigger surprise in the quarter-final tie against Eusebio's Portuguese. Having taken a shock lead in the first minute at Goodison Park, the North Koreans promptly doubled it, then scored a third to lead 3–0 with barely 25 minutes gone.

With his dream of World Cup glory slipping fast, it was Eusebio himself who took a decisive grip on proceedings. First, he scored a magnificent solo goal to bring Portugal back into the match then, just before half time, he converted a penalty after Torres was brought crashing down in the box. In the second half, Eusebio was untouchable, scoring two more goals – including a second penalty – and setting up a fifth to send Portugal through to a semi-final clash with England.

The day, however, belonged to the gallant North Koreans who, having already won an army of supporters in Middlesbrough, now counted the people of Liverpool among their most fervent admirers.

NORTH KOREA DISAPPOINT

They were the stars of the 1966 World Cup, but four years later North Korea were absent from the finals in Mexico. Indeed they were unceremoniously booted out of the qualifying rounds by FIFA after refusing to play Israel.

RECORD ATTENDANCE

The game between Brazil and Paraguay at the Maracana Stadium in Rio de Janeiro on 31 August 1969 attracted 183,341 spectators – a record for a World Cup qualifying game.

A PUZZLING DECISION

There have been many head-scratching decisions by World Cup referees, but perhaps none as baffling – or as suspicious – as that by Egypt's Ali Kandil during a group game between Mexico and El Salvador in 1970. Having awarded a free kick to El Salvador, Kandil then proceeded to watch as Mexico's Padilla took the kick and found his teammate Valdivia, who promptly scored. Despite the understandable protests of the El Salvadorians, Kandil refused to change his mind. Demoralised at what they perceived as blatant favouritism towards the hosts, El Salvador collapsed in the second half and lost 4–0.

MEXICO HELPED OUT AGAIN?

Having already benefited from a highly dubious refereeing decision in their 1970 group game against El Salvador, hosts Mexico continued to enjoy the largesse of the man in black in their next game against Belgium. Striker Valdivia seemed the only one to blame when, running into the Belgian penalty area, he tripped and fell over the prostrate Jeck, who had been laid out in a previous challenge. Unbelievably, the Argentinian referee awarded the spot kick, which Pena gleefully converted to give Mexico a 1–0 and winning lead.

BOBBY AND THE BRACELET

It seemed barely credible, but in May 1970, on a stop-over in Colombia en route to the 1970 finals in Mexico, England's upstanding captain Booby Moore found himself under arrest for the suspected theft of an emerald bracelet from a local shop. Despite international protests, Moore was detained under house arrest in Bogotá while the legal teams of both countries got to work. The case itself was a travesty: the chief witness to the alleged crime turned out to be the owner of a jewellery shop and not a passer-by as he first stated; Moore's chief accuser, shop assistant Clara Padilla, fled to the USA before she could be cross-examined; and the shop owner Danilo Rojas claimed £6,000 damages for a bracelet that cost £600. Indeed the whole scam was something that tourists regularly found themselves falling victim to.

Typically phlegmatic, Moore organised practice kick-arounds involving himself, the guards and the local children. This made him immensely popular with the Colombians, who pressured for his release. After four days under arrest, he was allowed to rejoin the rest of the squad in Mexico before the charges were eventually dropped. The case wasn't officially closed for five years, during which time Moore said that whenever he walked into a jewellery shop 'I have to keep my hands behind my back and point with my nose'.

PELÉ MAKES A POINT

Having been rough-housed out of the 1966 finals, Pelé had threatened to boycott the 1970 finals in Mexico – indeed he had even threatened to retire altogether. Fortunately, he changed his mind and, at the age of 29, became the fulcrum of one of the finest teams ever to play in the World Cup. It did not take long for the master to make his point: in the first group game against Czechoslovakia, Pelé saw the goalkeeper Viktor off his line and, from all of 60 yards, lazily lobbed it over his head. Fortunately for Viktor, the ball missed the post by inches.

SNIFFER'S BIG DAY

11 June 1970 was a day to remember for Leeds' Allan Clarke. Not only was it his birthday and his wedding anniversary, but he made his England debut in the group match against Czechoslovakia and scored the winner from the penalty spot.

RAISING THE CROWD

Keen to promote the 1970 tournament as the best ever, the Mexican football authorities routinely added thousands to the official attendances of even the most mundane matches.

	Official Attendance	Real Attendance
Belgium vs El Salvador	92,205	30,000
USSR vs El Salvador	89,970	25,000
England vs Czechoslovakia	49,292	35,000
Peru vs Morocco	13,537	7,000
Bulgaria vs Morocco	12,299	400
Uruguay vs USSR	96,085	45,000
West Germany vs Uruguay	104,403	32,000

POLITICAL DEFEAT

Labour Prime Minister Harold Wilson blamed England's shock 3–2 quarter-final defeat against West Germany in 1970 for his own defeat in the General Election that year. Prior to the match, the Labour party were seven points ahead in the polls. But four days later Ted Heath swept to power in the second shock result of the week.

UNLUCKY BELGIUM

During their qualifying campaign for the 1974 World Cup, Belgium beat Iceland 4–0 home and away, Norway 2–0 home and away, and drew 0–0 with Johan Cruyff's Holland in Antwerp. The return fixture against the Dutch was to be held in Amsterdam and, with both sides on nine points, a win for either side would see them qualify at the other's expense. In the event of a draw, goal difference would decide the issue. The match finished 0–0, which meant that the Dutch, having scored more goals against Norway and Iceland, went through. Unbeaten Belgium, despite scoring 12 goals and conceding 0, were nevertheless eliminated.

ELIMINATED

So much for the form book; four of the eight quarter-finalists in the 1966 tournament – Portugal, Hungary, North Korea and Argentina – failed to qualify for the finals in Mexico in 1970.

TWO YELLOWS DOES NOT NECESSARILY EQUAL A RED

The game between Australia and Chile in Berlin in 1974 was a dire 0–0 draw played by two poor sides who had no hope of progressing beyond the first round. Yet thanks to the differing approach of two referees, the match finds itself – perhaps undeservingly – in the history books. After 37 minutes, Iranian referee Jafar Namdar booked Australia's Ray Richards. Later on in the game, when Richards committed another foul, everyone in the Olympic stadium expected him to be sent off. Instead, whether by accident or design, Namdar brandished another yellow card and allowed him to play on. This outrageous bending of the rules proved too much for reserve referee Clive Thomas of Wales. Thomas, a man who once booked Coventry City's Roy Barry even as he was being stretchered off the pitch with a broken leg, ran down from the stands and informed the linesman of the situation. Namdar was alerted, and Richards was duly sent off – five minutes after receiving his second yellow.

A similarly infamous incident occurred at the 2006 World Cup, during the Group F Croatia vs Australia match on 22 June. After already sending off two players, Graham Poll failed to send off Croatian defender Josip Šimunic for a second yellow card late in the match (despite vociferous protests from the

Australian players), eventually sending him off for a third yellow for dissent at the final whistle. The match ended 2–2, and Australia progressed to the next round, but FIFA chief Sepp Blatter later commented that 'had Australia lost the game and gone out of the World Cup, they would have had grounds to request a replay'. Unsurprisingly, Poll was one of the 14 officials dismissed by FIFA from the remaining World Cup matches, and, suitably embarrassed, he boarded the plane home, his international refereeing career effectively over.

A SECOND YELLOW FOR CRUYFF

With his side trailing 2–1 at half time in the 1974 World Cup final, Dutch captain Johan Cruyff left the pitch moaning about some of the industrial-strength tackling he had been subjected to by the West Germans. His complaining earned him a yellow card from English referee Jack Taylor. In 1999, 25 years after the match, Cruyff and Taylor met again. This time the venue was Barcelona, where Cruyff was due to present Taylor with an award signifying his admittance to the FIFA International Hall of Fame. As he approached the stage, Taylor reached into his pocket and produced a yellow card, which he waved at Cruyff. Needless to say, the great Dutchman – and everyone else in the auditorium – saw the funny side.

IT'S A DOG'S LIFE FOR ALLY

With his world crumbling around him following a 3–1 defeat against Peru and a dismal 1–1 draw with Iran in the 1978 finals, Scotland boss Ally MacLeod was in reflective mood as he entertained the press at the team's hotel in Cordoba. 'I've few friends left now,' he informed the assembled hacks. At that moment a stray mongrel dog emerged from the undergrowth and trotted up to MacLeod. 'In fact the only friend I have is this wee brown dog,' MacLeod said, reaching down to stroke the animal – who promptly sank his fangs into the Scottish manager's thumb.

SMOKERS

Gerson, Brazil's influential midfielder in the 1970 World Cup, smoked three packets of cigarettes a day. Socrates, captain in 1982 and 1986, was a forty-a-day man, as was Osvaldo Ardiles of Argentina in 1978.

WORST KEEPER

Dimbi Tubilandu, Zaire's reserve goalkeeper, came on as a substitute 21 minutes into his side's 1974 group game against Yugoslavia. Zaire were already trailing 3–0, and the unfortunate Tubilandu went on to concede a further six as the Yugoslavs ran riot 9–0. Not only were those 69 minutes the only action Tubilandu saw in the tournament, but those seven goals make him the worst World Cup goalkeeper of all time. Harsh, perhaps – but statistics do not lie.

SEND IN THE CLOWN

Poland's goalkeeper Jan Tomaszewski was famously dismissed as a 'clown' by Brian Clough prior to a heroic performance at Wembley that resulted in England failing to qualify for the 1974 World Cup finals in West Germany. Any remaining doubts about his talent were swiftly dismissed in the finals themselves, as Tomaszewski made two penalty saves out of three in the second group stage, which helped propel his side as far as the third-place playoff. Here Tomaszewski kept a clean sheet against Brazil as the Poles won 1–0.

GOLDEN SALENKO

Few people had even heard of Russia's Oleg Salenko before the 1994 World Cup, let alone expected him to be joint winner of the Golden Boot award for top goalscorer. He ended up with six, alongside Bulgaria's Hristo Stoichkov – thanks largely to scoring five against Cameroon. Had the Russians not been eliminated, he may well have gone on to become the first player for twenty years to score more than six goals in a World Cup tournament.

GREAT GOALS

In 2000, visitors to the Planet World Cup website were asked to vote for the greatest World Cup goal. Here is their Top Ten:

DIEGO MARADONA, ARGENTINA VS ENGLAND, 1986

Having benefited from the 'Hand of God' to put Argentina ahead against England, Maradona then proved that he was truly blessed from above with a sensational second. Collecting the ball in the centre circle, the Argentine skipper turned on a sixpence and set off on a run straight at the England defence, leaving Peter Reid, Terry Fenwick and Terry Butcher bamboozled, before clipping the ball insolently past Peter Shilton.

SAEED OWAIRAN, SAUDI ARABIA VS BELGIUM, 1994

Owairan was known as the Maradona of the Arabs, and he showed why with a quite stunning, mazy run from the edge of his own penalty area that culminated in a thunderous strike for goal. In the past, Saudi players had been offered Rolls-Royces and Ferraris for World Cup success – so we can only guess what gifts were showered on Owairan after this brilliant solo goal.

ARIE HAAN, HOLLAND VS ITALY, 1978

There seemed little danger when Holland midfielder Arie Haan took possession from a free kick just inside the Italian half. But earlier in the competition Haan had blasted a 30-yard thunderbolt which left West Germany's Sepp Maier helpless, and now the Dutchman hit a scarcely credible shot from 40 yards which flew in off a post, leaving veteran keeper Dino Zoff scratching his head.

PELÉ, BRAZIL VS SWEDEN, 1958

The 17-year-old announced his presence on the world stage with a world-class goal in the 1958 final. As the cross came in from the left, he controlled the ball instantly on his knee, then flipped it nonchalantly over the defender's head before driving it into the back of the net.

ROBERTO BAGGIO, ITALY VS CZECHOSLOVAKIA, 1990

Pure genius from Baggio, who ran all the way from the halfway line, leaving the Czech defenders in his wake, before planting the ball in the back of the net.

DENNIS BERGKAMP, HOLLAND VS ARGENTINA, 1998

Sublime artistry from Bergkamp as he controlled de Boer's 50-yard pass with his right foot, stepped away from the Argentine defender, and then curled it with precision into the far corner of the net with his left.

DIEGO MARADONA, ARGENTINA VS BELGIUM, 1986

There is no such thing as a one-man team, but in 1986 it seemed that Maradona was running the entire World Cup to his own agenda. This goal, although not quite as good as his second against England, was still breathtaking. Again, the little man seemed to thrive on running directly at defenders, beating them and then scoring. Here he took on four Belgians before choosing the perfect moment to clip the ball past the advancing Pfaff.

ARCHIE GEMMILL, SCOTLAND VS HOLLAND, 1978

Scotland saved the best till last in their woeful 1978 campaign. Gemmill picked up a loose ball on the right of the Dutch penalty area, came inside Jansen's lunge, beat Krol on the outside, nutmegged Poortvliet then delicately chipped it over the advancing keeper. A brilliant goal, but sadly too little too late for Ally MacLeod's men.

Gemmill

CARLOS ALBERTO, BRAZIL VS ITALY, 1970

Already leading 3–1 in the final, this was the icing on the cake for the brilliant Brazilians. After tricky footwork by Clodoaldo, the ball finally reached Pelé on the edge of the box. His perfect lay-off found the skipper steaming up the right-hand channel, and his thunderous shot was unstoppable.

MANUEL NEGRETE, MEXICO VS BULGARIA, 1986

Controlling a difficult bouncing ball with ease on the edge of the area, Negrete played a neat one-two before bursting the net with a stunning mid-air scissor kick from the edge of the box.

GOLDEN BOOTS

The scorer of the most goals in a tournament is awarded the coveted Golden Boot. The winners since 1930 have been:

1930	Guilermo Stabile (ARG) 8
1934	Oldrich Nejedly (CZE), Angelo Schiavo (ITA); Edmund Conen (GER) 4
1938	Leonidas (BRA)...8
1950	Ademir (BRA) 9
1954	Sandor Kocsis (HUN)................................ 11
1958	Juste Fontaine (FRA)................................. 13
1962	Garrincha (BRA), Valentin Ivanov (SOV), Leonel Sanchez (CHI), Florian Albert (HUN), Vava (BRA), Drazan Jerkovic (YUG) 4
1966	Eusebio (POR)..9
1970	Gerd Muller (GER) 10
1974	Gzegorz Lato (POL) 7
1978	Mario Kempes (ARG) 6
1982	Paolo Rossi (ITA) 6
1986	Gary Lineker (ENG) 6
1990	Salvatore Schillaci (ITA) 6
1994	Hristo Stoichkov (BUL), Oleg Salenko (RUS)......6
1998	Davor Suker (CRO)......................................6
2002	Ronaldo (BRA)...8
2006	Miroslav Klose (GER) 5
2010	Thomas Muller (GER)................................. *

* Muller's five goals were equalled by Spain's David Villa, Diego Forlan of Uruguay and Wesley Sneijder of Holland, but the German was awarded the Golden Boot by virtue of having the most assists (3).

MOST GOALS IN ONE MATCH

5 Oleg Salenko (RUS) vs Cameroon, 1994
4 Emilio Butragueno (SPA) vs Denmark, 1986
4 Eusebio (POR) vs North Korea, 1966
4 Juste Fontaine (FRA) vs West Germany, 1958
4 Sandor Kocsis (HUN) vs West Germany, 1954
4 Ademir (BRA) vs Sweden, 1950
4 Juan Schiaffino (URU) vs Bolivia, 1950
4 Leonidas (BRA) vs Poland, 1938
4 Ernst Willimowski (POL) vs Brazil, 1938
4 Gustav Wetterstrom (SWE) vs Cuba, 1938

LANDMARK GOALS

1st Lucien Laurent (FRA) v Mexico, 1930
500th Bobby Collins (SCO) v Paraguay, 1958
1000th Robbie Rensenbrink (HOL) v Scotland, 1978
1500th Claudio Caniggia (ARG) v Nigeria, 1994
2000th Marcus Allback (SWE) v England, 2006
2208th Andres Iniesta (SPA) v Holland, 2010

TOP TEN SHOCKING RESULTS

ENGLAND 0–1 USA, 1950
Billy Wright and co were humiliated by American part-timers.

NORTH KOREA 1–0 ITALY, 1966
Fans pelted the Azzurri with rotten tomatoes after this horror show at Ayresome Park.

ALGERIA 2–1 WEST GERMANY, 1986
The 1,000–1 outsiders beat the 3–1 favourites. 'I still can't believe this,' said German boss Jupp Derwall. 'It is beyond my understanding.'

CAMEROON 1–0 ARGENTINA, 1990
Nine-man Cameroon ran Diego Maradona's men ragged.

SENEGAL 1–0 FRANCE, 2002
The reigning World Champions humbled by minnows making their first appearance in the tournament.

EAST GERMANY 1–0 WEST GERMANY, 1974
The first meeting between the two teams, and a major upset.

SPAIN 5–1 DENMARK, 1986
Denmark had cruised through the group and were leading this match before a dramatic and inexplicable collapse.

BULGARIA 2–1 GERMANY, 1994
Germany are leading 1–0 and heading for the semi-finals when Stoitchkov and Letchkov pounce with two goals in two minutes.

NORTHERN IRELAND 1–0 SPAIN, 1982
The hosts are silenced by Gerry Armstrong's emphatic winner.

SOUTH AFRICA 2–1 FRANCE, 2010
France had been teetering on the brink of self-destruction all tournament. This defeat at the hands of an exuberant Bafana Bafana was the final nail in the coffin of the 1998 World Cup winners.

MOROCCO MAGIC

In reaching the 1970 finals in Mexico, Morocco became the first African side to qualify since Egypt in 1934. And as 500–1 outsiders, they surely deserved more assistance than they received from Dutch referee Laurens van Ravens during their group game with West Germany. Leading a goal to nil, and playing an energetic style of football which had the supposedly superior Europeans rattled, Morocco took to the field for the second half with just ten men while goalkeeper Allal Ben Kassu received some last-minute instructions in the tunnel. To their horror, referee van Ravens blew for the restart and, despite Moroccan protests, let the game continue for over a minute before allowing Kassu back onto the pitch. It was testament to how badly the Germans were playing that they failed even to get a shot in during that time – and that they were relieved to finally run out 2–1 winners.

BECKENBAUER'S SHOULDER

West Germany's inspirational Franz Beckenbauer played for more than an hour of his side's epic 1970 semi-final against Italy with a dislocated shoulder.

HOME ADVANTAGE

Uruguay complained that Brazil would have home advantage in their World Cup semi-final in 1970 – even though the match was played in Guadalajara, Mexico!

CUP HOLDERS

If it were needed, there was an extra spice to the 1970 World Cup final between Italy and Brazil in Mexico. As both teams had won the tournament twice, the winner this time would be allowed to keep the trophy in perpetuity. Brazil, of course, won 4–1.

OPEN GOAL

Chile were favourites to qualify for the 1974 World Cup finals in Germany after travelling to Moscow and securing a 0–0 draw in the first leg of their tie against the Soviet Union. And their progress was put beyond all doubt when the Soviets refused to play the second leg. The match was due to be played at the National Stadium in Santiago, but the Soviets complained that the stadium had been used to house thousands of political prisoners when the Chilean military overthrew the Marxist government of President Salvador Allende. Unconcerned with this, FIFA ordered that the match should go ahead. Chile duly kicked off and scored in the empty Soviet net to secure the easiest win in World Cup history.

MARXIST MARKSMAN

During their opening game of the 1974 World Cup against the hosts West Germany, the Chile team found itself the target of barracking from a section of Marxist sympathisers in the crowd. The protesters were complaining about the right-wing military coup that had resulted in the overthrow of the democratically elected Marxist government of Salvador Allende. It must have been particularly satisfying, therefore, that the winning goal was scored by Germany's Paul Breitner – himself an avowed Marxist.

EAST VS WEST

The historic first clash between East and West Germany took place at Hamburg's Volkspark Stadium in 1974. The match was a 60,000 sell-out – although only 3,000 of that number had been granted permission to cross the border following strict security vetting. It was they who had the last laugh, however, as the East ran out 1–0 victors thanks to a late goal by Sparwasser.

ZAIRE SPIT THE DUMMY

After losing 9–0 and having a man sent off against Yugoslavia, Zaire were so disheartened they decided to go home from the 1974 World Cup in Germany. Only some frantic behind-the-scenes negotiation by FIFA officials persuaded them to stay. They did – only to lose 3–0 to Brazil.

HAITI DOPE

Having taken a shock lead against Italy during a group match in 1974, the minnows of Haiti won widespread praise by only losing by 3–1. However, the Haitian 'management' showed little goodwill when one of their players, Ernst Jean-Joseph, became the first player in World Cup history to be tested positive for drugs. The unfortunate Joseph was sent home in disgrace – having first been dragged from the team's base and beaten up by hired thugs loyal to the dictator 'Papa Doc' Duvalier.

WO IST DIE CORNER FLAGS?

Before an assembled crowd of 77,833 at Munich's Olympic Stadium, and an estimated worldwide television audience of one billion, Jack Taylor, the English referee, was about to start the 1974 World Cup final between West Germany and Holland – when he noticed the corner flags were missing!

THE ONE-MINUTE PENALTY

Holland took the lead in the 1974 World Cup final against West Germany with a penalty by Johan Neeskens after just one minute. In that time the Dutch had kicked off and completed a movement of sixteen passes before Cruyff was brought down in the penalty box. Amazingly, not one German player had even touched the ball.

NO KIDNAPPINGS TODAY

Argentina were awarded the 1978 World Cup finals as far back as 1966, when the country was seen as a model of peaceful democracy. Twelve years later, it was run by a brutal military junta and riven with violent insurrection by left-wing terrorists. It was only when the revolutionaries agreed to suspend their programme of killings and kidnappings because 'football is a game of the working class' that FIFA agreed to let the tournament commence.

GRASS KILLER

With just weeks to go before the 1978 World Cup in Argentina, a groundsman at the River Plate stadium in Buenos Aires decided to sprinkle the pitch with sea water. Not surprisingly, the grass promptly died, resulting in the whole pitch having to be returfed.

HEFTY BILL FOR THE JUNTA

The right-wing Argentinian junta were so determined to make the 1978 World Cup a showpiece, they spent an estimated £500 million ($700 million) on building stadiums and making existing grounds fit for the tournament. The expenditure also included hiring a public relations firm, razing slums and moving the poor to areas where they wouldn't be visible to the thousands of foreign media and visitors.

CHANGE STRIPS

Aware that in 1978 many of the estimated one billion television viewers would be watching on black-and-white sets, FIFA ordered France (blue) and Hungary (red) to play their group match in change strips. Unfortunately, both teams turned up in all-white kit – resulting in an embarrassing 40-minute delay before a replacement set could be found and the match could kick off.

RARE GOAL

Erwin Vandenbergh's winning goal for Belgium against Argentina in the 1982 finals in Spain was the first to be scored in an inaugural match since 1962. It was also the first time the defending champions had lost their opening match since Italy in 1950.

REFEREEING DECISION

Sweden and Brazil were playing out a largely uninspiring 1–1 draw in their opening group match of the 1978 finals in Argentina when, in the dying seconds, the Brazilians won a corner. The ball was flighted in by Nelinho and forcefully headed home by Zico – but the Brazilian celebrations were short-lived. In one of the more controversial – not to say pedantic – decisions in World Cup history, Welsh referee Clive Thomas had blown for full time the moment Nelinho had struck the dead ball.

DOPE TEST

It seemed like adding insult to injury when, having been on the end of a humiliating defeat to Peru in the first game of the 1978 World Cup campaign, Scotland's Willie Johnston was drug tested and found positive for the stimulant fencamfamine. The news provoked one Scottish journalist to remark that Johnston's display in the match was 'so utterly lethargic that one has to seriously question the efficacy of the drug.' Johnston was sent home, protesting that drug taking was standard practice at his club, West Bromwich Albion. His comments led to a major investigation by the Football League, and the introduction of random dope testing for English clubs.

SMILE PLEASE, HUGO

Mexico's Hugo Sanchez, a star of the 1986 tournament, was not only a natural goalscorer, he was also a qualified dentist!

HUNGARY FOR GOALS

It is one of the great perversities of the World Cup that Hungary failed to win the 1954 tournament, despite scoring a record 27 goals in just five matches, including nine against South Korea, eight against West Germany, and four apiece against Brazil and Uruguay.

FIX?

As hosts of the 1978 tournament, Argentina had played well but still found themselves needing to beat Peru by four clear goals to reach the final ahead of arch rivals Brazil. On paper, it seemed an impossible task — but to everyone's astonishment Argentina went on to score six against a strong side who had not conceded more than three goals in any match in the tournament to that point. Surprise quickly turned to suspicion when it was revealed that Admiral Carlos Lacoste, a high-ranking member of the Argentine junta who had served as World Cup organiser and Vice-President of FIFA, had subsequently arranged for 35,000 tons of free grain to be transported to Peru, and that the Argentine Central Bank had unfrozen around $50 million in credits to the Peruvian government. Although Peru's Argentine-born goalkeeper Carlos Quiroga published an open letter defending himself and his team, it did not dispel the notion that the hosts had reached the final courtesy of one of the most outrageous match fixes of all time.

PLASTER CAST

The 1978 World Cup final between Argentina and Holland was billed as a spectacular clash of the best South America and Europe could offer. But no sooner had the ticker tape been thrown from the towering stands of the River Plate stadium than the match was plunged into controversy. First, the Dutch were left waiting on the pitch for five minutes before the hosts arrived. Then the Argentinians took exception to a small plaster cast which Holland's Rene van der Kerkhof was wearing on his forearm, the result of an injury sustained in the first match. When the Italian referee, Sergio Gonella, upheld the protest, the Dutch threatened to walk off the pitch. (Gonella himself was only selected as referee because the Argentinians had objected to the first choice, an Israeli who, they claimed, had links to the Dutch side.)

A compromise was eventually reached when van der Kerkhof agreed to play with a soft covering on his cast, but Holland were rattled and went on to lose their second successive World Cup final 3–1 in extra time.

DRAW FARCE

Spain spent in excess of £60 million on staging the 1982 World Cup. It's just a pity a few quid couldn't have been spent on ensuring the draw for the finals ran smoothly. Watched by an incredulous global TV audience, the list of cock-ups included:

- ⚽ England were one of the six top seeds, despite the fact they had finished second in their qualifying group and struggled to reach the finals.
- ⚽ To prevent Peru and Chile from appearing in the same group as South American rivals Brazil and Argentina, the miniature footballs containing their names were supposed to be left out of the metal cage used to make the draw. Somebody forgot to leave them out.
- ⚽ Scotland were drawn in Argentina's group before it was realised it should have been Belgium. The Scots were drawn again, this time in Brazil's group.
- ⚽ The metal cage jammed, snapping one of the miniature footballs in half.

ROSSI'S TRIUMPHANT RETURN

One of the stars of the 1978 tournament, Paolo Rossi of Italy, was the winner of the Golden Boot four years later in Spain. But then it was the first time he had appeared for the Azzurri in two years following a ban for match-fixing. While on loan with Perugia in 1980, Rossi was accused of taking a bribe after scoring both goals in a 2–2 draw with Avellino. Although initially suspended for three years, a combination of the striker's protests and the Italian side's dire need for a marksman meant that the sentence was commuted to two years, ending conveniently in April 1982 — just two months before the start of the tournament.

ROUT

With civil war raging back home, it was perhaps understandable that El Salvador had other things on their mind rather than a World Cup finals group match against Hungary in 1982. Sadly, Hungary were in no mood for sympathy and won 10–1, a record in World Cup finals. Such was the dominance of the Hungarians that three of the goals were scored by Lazlo Kiss, who came on as a substitute after 55 minutes and duly wrapped up his hat trick in seven minutes, another World Cup record.

GREAT GAMES: England 3–2 Cameroon (aet), 1990

Having already reduced their supporters' nerves to shreds against Belgium, England once again put the Barmy Army through the wringer in what was expected to be a walkover against Cameroon in the quarter-final. Platt gave them the lead on 25 minutes, but England were then comprehensively outplayed by the Africans, who could have easily scored three goals in the first half. With the iconic Roger Milla on in the second, Cameroon scored twice in five minutes to put Bobby Robson's men on the brink of an ignominious exit. They were saved by an 83rd minute Lineker penalty which took the match into extra time, then by a second Lineker spot kick with just six minutes remaining. Cameroon were out, but England were lucky.

ROBSON'S RECORD BREAKER

After a shaky qualification, England weren't expected to set World Cup 1982 alight – especially when key players Kevin Keegan and Trevor Brooking were ruled out of the first-group match against France with injuries. Inspirational midfielder Bryan Robson had other ideas, however. With just 27 seconds on the clock, Robson latched onto a cross to hammer the ball into the net. It launched England on their way to a marvellous 3–1 victory and an unbeaten record in the group. But as so often, England had flattered to deceive. Having drawn against West Germany in the second-group phase, they needed to beat Spain by two clear goals to reach the semi-finals. Forced to field the clearly unfit Keegan and Brooking, England crashed out of the tournament following a nerve-wracking goalless draw.

BANNED CAPTAIN

Luigi Allemandi captained Italy in the 1934 World Cup – despite having been banned from the game for life after accepting a 50,000-lire bribe to throw a league match between Juventus and Torino. As one of their best players, the selectors decided it would be prudent to rehabilitate Allemandi rather than lose him for the finals.

THE DEATH OF A LEGEND

The 20,000 Scottish fans who descended on Ninian Park for their side's World Cup qualifying match against Wales on 15 September 1985 were jubilant after Davy Cooper's 81st-minute penalty secured the draw they needed for Mexico. But on the touchline, manager Jock Stein had collapsed after an altercation with a photographer near the dug-out. Stein was rushed to the dressing room where, after an agonising wait of nearly twenty minutes, it was announced to a stunned crowd that the Big Man had died.

ARMSTRONG POUNCES

In 1958 Billy Bingham played for Northern Ireland in the World Cup finals in Sweden, so after an absence of 24 years it was perhaps fitting that Bingham should be the manager to take the Irish to the finals in Spain. Few expected them to qualify from a strong group and, after a brave draw against Yugoslavia and a more fitful stalemate against Honduras, it was assumed their final match against the hosts would be their swansong in the competition. The Irish, though, had other ideas. In front of a partisan crowd of 50,000 in Valencia, Bingham's men were immediately under the cosh. Then, two minutes before half time, Spanish keeper Arconada lethargically palmed away a cross by Billy Hamilton and there was striker Gerry Armstrong to lash home the rebound. Despite having Mal Donaghy sent off on the hour for retaliating to a crunching tackle by Camacho, the Irish somehow clung on for a win, which, against all the odds, saw them through to the next phase as group winners.

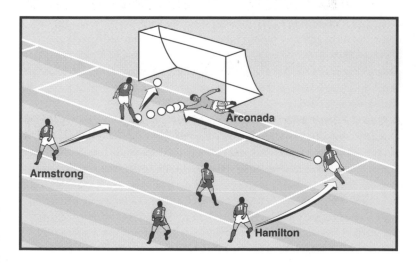

THE PRINCE STEPS IN

Trailing 3–1 to a Michel Platini-inspired French team, the minnows of Kuwait were heading out of the 1982 World Cup. And that might well have been the last we heard of them, had it not been for an extraordinary incident after 76 minutes. With the Kuwaiti defence seemingly playing statues in the penalty area, Alain Giresse nipped in to make it 4–1 from close range. As Giresse celebrated, the Kuwaitis surrounded Soviet referee Stupar claiming that they had stopped after hearing a whistle. The situation exploded into farce seconds later when none other than Prince Fahid, the Kuwaiti FA president, marched onto the pitch and demanded that the goal should be disallowed. For eight minutes a furious row took place in which the Prince threatened to take his players off the pitch and French boss Michel Hidalgo had to be restrained by the police when the referee subsequently reversed his decision.

With order finally, if unsatisfactorily, restored, the match restarted. Bossis scored to make it 4–1 again. This time Prince Fahid had no cause for complaint – and it is unlikely the £8,000 FIFA fine troubled his bank balance either.

BRAZIL GOALS

Brazil lit up the 1982 World Cup finals in Spain with some extraordinary goals. Among the highlights were:

- ⚽ **Brazil 2–1 Soviet Union:** Socrates equalises with a thunderous long-range shot before a swerving left-foot effort by Eder clinches the win.
- ⚽ **Brazil 4–1 Scotland** Zico bamboozles Rough with a viciously curling free kick from the edge of the box before Eder leaves the Scottish keeper stranded with an exquisite lob.
- ⚽ **Brazil 4–0 New Zealand** Zico opens the scoring with an improbable bicycle kick straight into the back of the net.
- ⚽ **Brazil 3–1 Argentina** Eder's long-range free kick dips and swerves before crashing off the underside of the bar for Zico to apply the finish. Junior then fires home after some sensational one-touch approach play which leaves the Argentines helpless.

✪ **Brazil 2–3 Italy** Brazil bow out, but not before Falcao scores one of the goals of the tournament, wrong-footing the defence before driving home a magnificent left-foot effort from the edge of the box.

IRELAND ELIMINATED

History repeated itself when Northern Ireland were eliminated from the 1982 finals in Spain thanks to a 4–1 defeat to France. In 1958, the last time the Irish appeared in the finals, they were knocked out by France, who scored four goals against them.

CAUSIO GETS HIS REWARD

With just minutes remaining in the World Cup final of 1982, and with his side leading West Germany 3–1, Italian manager Enzo Bearzot substituted goalscorer Altobelli and replaced him with Franco Causio, thus ensuring the veteran would receive a winners' medal.

COLOMBIA BALE OUT

Colombia was the original choice as venue for the 1986 World Cup finals, but when they couldn't raise the finances required FIFA moved the tournament to Mexico for the second time.

REPEAT PERFORMANCE FROM HURST

As a fundraiser for victims of the Bradford fire disaster in 1985, members of the 1966 England World Cup-winning team arranged a match with their German counterparts at Elland Road, Leeds. This time England won 6–4 – and 46-year-old Geoff Hurst got another hat trick.

ON YOUR BIKE, PEDRO

Fanatical Argentina supporter Pedro Garita was determined to see his team play in the 1986 World Cup in Mexico. Lacking the money for the airfare, he decided to travel there by bicycle. He arrived a month later, having covered 4,460 miles, in time for the final between Argentina and West Germany. Unfortunately, Pedro approached the ticket office to be told the match was a sell-out and had been for weeks. To make matters worse, as he trudged disconsolately outside, he discovered that someone had nicked his bike!

BATISTUTA HAT TRICKS

On 21 June 1994, Argentina striker Gabriel Batistuta scored a penalty to complete a hat trick against Greece, who were competing in their first World Cup finals. On 21 June 1998 Batistuta scored a penalty to complete a hat trick against Jamaica, who were competing in their first World Cup finals.

UNPOPULAR HARALD

After his horror tackle on Patrick Battiston in the 1982 semi-final against France, West German goalkeeper Harald Schumacher was voted the 'most unpopular man in history' in a French newspaper poll. Adolf Hitler came second.

BLUNDER SQUAD

Everyone likes to speculate on the all-time greatest World Cup players – but what about the players who had the worst moments in the World Cup? Here's a squad of unfortunates you wouldn't like to see in your team colours.

 Goalkeeper Andoni Zubizarreta (Spain). Literally handed a 3–2 victory to Nigeria when a pair of blunders cost his team a second-round berth in 1998.

Defenders José Batista (Uruguay) received the fastest red card in Cup history after 53 seconds in a 1986 match. Barmeer Shaker (Iraq) was handed a one-year suspension for spitting at a referee after a defeat to Belgium in 1986. Rigobert Song (Cameroon) is the only player to be red-carded in two Cups, in 1994 and 1998.

Midfielders Ray Wilkins (England) was sent off for throwing the ball at the referee during a match against Morocco in 1986. Stefan Effenberg (Germany) was sent home after giving a one-fingered salute to fans after a game in 1994. Ariel Ortega (Argentina) was red-carded for head-butting keeper Edwin Van Der Sar, minutes before Holland's winning goal in 1998.

Forwards Hugo Sanchez (Mexico) missed a penalty kick in a 1–1 draw with Paraguay in 1986 after he was featured in a TV commercial converting a kick. Gianluca Vialli (Italy) missed a penalty kick, had a goal disallowed due to offside and missed a sitter with an embarrassingly poor bicycle kick during a match against the USA in 1990.

Coach Paraguay's Cayeteano Re became the first coach to be ejected from a match, in 1986. His crime? Standing too close to the field.

ZOLA'S BIRTHDAY

Italy striker Gianfranco Zola was hoping to celebrate his 28th birthday with a World Cup win against Nigeria in the 1994 finals. His side duly won 2–1, but Zola's happy day was soured when he was sent off after 76 minutes.

PREUD'HOMME'S SHIRT

During the 1994 finals in America Belgian goalkeeper Michael Preud'homme never forgot his roots, and underneath his international jersey always wore a Standard Liège shirt in homage to his first club and to bring him good luck. Unfortunately, having qualified for the knock-out phases, Preud'homme decided it was just too hot to wear two shirts and left his Liège jersey in the changing room for the match against Germany. Inevitably, the Germans put three goals past him to win 3–2.

ALBANIA SHIRTS

After a qualifying tie with Spain in 1993, Albania coach Bekjush Berce forbade his players from exchanging shirts. The reason was that the Albanian FA only had eleven shirts, and were so impoverished they couldn't afford a new set.

ROMANIA PLAY BY ROYAL APPOINTMENT

Romania's players attended the 1930 World Cup finals by royal command – literally. The team was hand-picked by soccer-mad King Carol II, who also ordered their employers to grant them three months leave on full pay.

EXTRA EXTRA TIME

There were puzzled looks between the players of Italy and Argentina as the first half of extra time in their 1990 semi-final dragged on for 23 minutes. Nobody had been injured, there had been no hold-ups, so why didn't French referee Michel Vautrot blow his whistle? It was only when one of the Italian players posed the question that the embarrassed Vautrot realised he had been so engrossed in the match he had forgotten to look at his watch. Fortunately, no goals were scored in the extra time of extra time.

MEXICO BANNED

Mexico, hosts of the 1986 finals, were banned from the 1990 tournament in Italy after FIFA discovered they had fielded three over-age players in an international youth tournament.

SIX MINUTES

When Brazilian referee Almeida Rega blew for full time in the 1930 match between Argentina and France, the South Americans were understandably jubilant. Not only were they clinging onto a 1–0 lead, but there were still six minutes to go. A red-faced Rega apologised and, half-an-hour later, brought the two sides back onto the pitch in order to play out the last six minutes. There were no further goals.

URUGUAY CAGED

Prior to staging the inaugural World Cup finals in 1930, the Uruguay squad were isolated in a Montevideo hotel for nearly eight weeks to ensure there were no distractions to their preparations. The regime proved too much for goalkeeper Antonio Mazzali, who staged a daring midnight break-out in order to visit his girlfriend.

ONE-HAND CASTRO

Hector Castro of Uruguay scored the winning goal in the 1930 final, despite having lost a hand and part of his arm in a childhood accident.

NEW HOUSE

Each member of the victorious Uruguay team of 1930 was given a plot of land and a new house in Montevideo by their grateful government.

POLDI MAKES A SPECTACLE OF HIMSELF

Swiss centre-forward Poldi Keilholz was so short-sighted he had to wear spectacles when he played. Nevertheless this did not prevent him banging in three goals in two matches during the 1934 finals.

WASTED JOURNEY

After a sea journey of more than 6,000 miles, Mexico and the USA arrived in Rome for the 1934 World Cup finals to be informed they must play a qualifying match to see which of them actually qualified for the finals. Mexico lost 4–2 and went home immediately. The USA lasted precisely three days longer, when they were beaten by the hosts in the first game of the finals!

AWESOME ORSI SHOT

Italian winger Raimondo Orsi's freakishly curling shot in the 1934 final against Czechoslovakia was worthy of winning any World Cup final. In reality Orsi's goal was the dramatic last-gasp equaliser which took the match into extra time which Italy went on to win. The following day, Orsi, accompanied by dozens of press photographers, returned to the stadium in order to reproduce the shot for posterity. Despite trying more than twenty times, however, the ball resolutely refused to find the back of the net. Eventually, Orsi gave up.

LEONIDAS STICKS THE BOOT IN

At the start of a 1938 finals match against Poland, Brazilian player Leonidas took off his boots because he wanted to play in the muddy pitch barefooted. The referee immediately ordered him to put his boots back on. The Polish players must have wished the ref had kept his mouth shut: Leonidas went on to score four goals in the match, and to finish top scorer in the competition with eight goals in four matches. It might have been more had he not been controversially rested for the semi-final against Italy – a match which the understrength Brazilians went on to lose 2–1.

BROTHERS IN MANAGEMENT

Brazil's 1954 manager Zeze and the side's 1962 boss Aimore Moreira are the only two brothers to have managed the same nation in World Cup finals.

PEPPINO'S SHORTS

Peppino Meazza of Italy was overjoyed to score a penalty in the 1938 World Cup semi-final. But his moment of glory quickly turned to humiliation when his shorts – which had been torn earlier in the match – gave up the ghost and fell to his ankles, revealing his bare backside to the capacity Rome crowd. Meazza's teammates surrounded him, protecting his shattered modesty until a replacement pair could be brought onto the pitch.

WIN OR DIE

Before the 1938 World Cup final against Hungary, the Italian team were sent a telegram by their dictator Mussolini, urging them to 'Win…or Die!' Fortunately for Italy, they did indeed win.

NO BRITISH TEAMS

British teams declined to enter the World Cup finals until 1950. This was because in 1928 the four home associations had quit FIFA over a row about so-called 'broken time' payments to amateur players. They did not rejoin FIFA until 1946.

RIMET HIDDEN

To prevent the Nazis from stealing the Jules Rimet trophy during the war, the World Cup was kept in a shoebox under the bed of Dr Ottorino Barrassi, an Italian sports official and member of FIFA's ruling council.

ENGLAND DEFEAT IS VICTORY

Early editions of British newspapers reported that England had beaten the USA 10–1 in the 1950 finals, when in fact the Americans had recorded a 1–0 win. The reason for the mistake was simple: sports editors refused to believe that England could have lost, and assumed the copy-takers had made a typing error.

WHATEVER HAPPENED TO LARRY?

Larry Gaetjens was born in Haiti, but became a hero in his adopted USA when he scored the goal which defeated England in the 1950 World Cup finals. Returning to Haiti after his career was over, Gaetjens became a political activist, and was responsible for organising several anti-government organisations. This eventually landed him in jail where, starved and tortured, he died. His body was never found.

IRON BAR

Making his way to the pitch for his country's match against Brazil in 1950, giant Yugoslav player Rajko Mitic smacked his head on an iron girder in a corridor of the half-built Maracana Stadium. With blood pouring from his wound, Mitic was taken away for stitches while the Yugoslav officials asked the referee to delay the kickoff by ten minutes. He refused, and so Yugoslavia took the field with just ten men. Brazil duly scored after three minutes. Despite a gallant rearguard action led by the heavily bandaged Mitic, the hosts ran out 2–0 winners.

HOLY DAY

Having qualified for the 1958 World Cup finals, Northern Ireland were very nearly scuppered by their own football association. Two of their pool games were scheduled to be played on Sunday which, the Northern Irish FA pointed out, was against Irish law. Incredibly, it took a vehement protest by the players themselves to persuade the FA to scrap the law and prevent the team being disqualified for not completing their matches.

LEONIDAS, P.I.

After becoming the top scorer in the 1938 finals, Brazilian striker Leonidas returned to Rio where he continued in his day job – as a private investigator.

IDENTITY CRISIS

The opening match of the 1966 World Cup between England and Uruguay suffered an administrative glitch because seven of the England team had left their identity tags at the hotel. A motorcycle dispatch rider was immediately sent back to get them.

SUDAN THROUGH

Despite both teams winning 4–2 in their qualifying matches, Sudan went through to the 1970 World Cup finals at Zambia's expense because of a FIFA directive that the team scoring more goals in the second leg – in this case Sudan – would go through. Unsurprisingly it was the first and only time this grossly unfair means of qualification was used.

RIVELINO STRETCHERED OFF

Having survived the clumsy challenges of clodhopping defenders to become one of the players of the 1970 World Cup, Brazil's Rivelino was eventually stretchered off the pitch at the end of the final against Italy – after being jumped on by his own jubilant supporters.

EYE FOR AN EYE

Having had his sight saved by an operation prior to the 1970 World Cup finals, Brazil's Tostao gratefully gave his winners' medal to his eye surgeon.

TWO CRACKERS BY JOSIMAR

For a player who was, according to the team sheet anyway, a full-back, Brazil's Josimar Pereira scored two of the best goals of the 1986 World Cup. His first came against Northern Ireland, and was a raking 25-yard drive which left 41-year-old Pat Jennings helpless. His second was even better: receiving the ball on the right against Poland, he dribbled through three tackles before blasting a viciously dipping shot over goalkeeper Mlynarczyk from a seemingly impossible angle.

FAMOUS LAST WORDS

After snootily claiming that the World Cup trophy would never be stolen in Brazil because its fans loved and respected the game too much, the Brazilian football authorities were left red-faced in 1983 when the Jules Rimet trophy, won in perpetuity in 1970, was duly nicked from a display cabinet at the BFA headquarters in Rio. It was never recovered – unlike in England, where Pickles the dog was the hero of the hour.

NEW TROPHY

Unlike the Jules Rimet trophy, the current FIFA World Cup trophy will not be given to the next team to win three tournaments. However, in 2038 all the space for the winners' names on the base of the trophy will have been used up – which means that the winners of the 2042 tournament will be the first to lift the new World Cup.

THE MADNESS OF EL LOCO

Known as El Loco ('The Madman'), Peru's goalkeeper Ramon Quiroga was well known for running out of his penalty area in order to help out his defence and, sometimes, his midfield. During a pool game against Poland in 1978, El Loco excelled even himself by racing fully 60 yards from his goal line and rugby-tackling winger Gzegorz Lato.

SCHUMACHER'S TACKLE

The semi-final of the 1982 World Cup between West Germany and France
will be for ever remembered for an act of brutality which was only topped
in the incredulity stakes by the refereeing decision which followed it. With
57 minutes played and the scores tied at 1–1, France's Patrick Battiston was
sent clean through the German defence. Harald Schumacher, Germany's
combative, permed goalkeeper came racing out of his goal and launched into
Battiston in what can only be described as a kung fu-style assault. Battiston
crashed to the turf, where he lay unconscious for three minutes, blood pouring
from his mouth where three of his teeth had been knocked out (Spanish
police had inexplicably banned the Red Cross from attending the game).
Unsurprisingly, the French team were incensed, and even Schumacher himself
seemed prepared for the inevitable dismissal. Yet, incredibly, Dutch referee
Charles Corver not only declined to book the goalkeeper, but awarded the
Germans a free kick! Corver claimed not to have seen the incident – which
would have made him the only one in the stadium.

LERBY'S PREVIOUS ENGAGEMENT

With his side cruising to a 4–1 victory in a qualifying match against the
Republic of Ireland in Dublin in 1985, Danish midfielder Soren Lerby was
substituted after 58 minutes. Instead of an early bath, however, Lerby was
driven to the airport where he caught a private jet to Munich – where he was
in time to come on as a substitute in his club Bayern's 1–1 draw against rivals
Bochum in a third-round cup game.

ROOSTER BOOSTER

During a match between France and Canada in 1986, the referee was obliged
to stop the match while a dead cockerel was removed from the pitch. It had
been thrown there by Canadian fans.

SPITTING MAD

Iraqi defender Barmeer Shaker was banned for a year by FIFA after spitting at the referee following his side's 2–1 defeat to Belgium in 1986.

EVEN STEVENS

There were two players called Gary Stevens in the England side that played Paraguay in 1986. They were not related.

ESCOBAR ASSASSINATED

Scoring an own goal is unfortunate, but it is hardly a capital offence. Yet that is precisely what happened to Colombia defender Andres Escobar in 1994. Playing against the USA, Escobar stuck out a leg to clear a cross by Harkes and put it past his own goalkeeper. The US went on to win the game 2–1, and were eventually eliminated from the tournament. Nine days later, Escobar was leaving a restaurant in Medellin with his fiancée when he was attacked by three men. One of them said 'Thanks for the own goal' and repeatedly shot Escobar in the chest and face. As each bullet struck home the assailants shouted: 'Goal'. Over 100,000 Colombians attended his funeral. A few months later Humberto Munoz Castro, a chauffeur, was arrested for the shooting. He was alleged to be a hitman acting for wealthy drug barons who had bet $20 million on Colombia beating the USA. On 30 June 1995, almost exactly a year after Escobar's own goal, Castro was jailed for 43 years.

WHO'S GOT THE BALL?

One of the great conundrums in the wake of the 1966 World Cup final was 'did the ball cross the line?' Another was: 'what actually happened to the ball?' It was generally assumed that as the scorer of a hat trick, the ball was in the possession of Geoff Hurst. Not so. In the build-up to Euro '96, it transpired that it was actually in the attic of Helmut Haller, scorer of the first

West German goal. 'It rolled towards me at the end and I picked it up,' Haller revealed. Thus began a concerted campaign by the English tabloid press to bring the ball back home. After several weeks of wrangling and underhand dealing, Haller and the ball were eventually smuggled into England by the Daily Mirror. The ball was placed at Waterloo Station and Haller was paid £70,000. Today the ball has pride of place at the National Football Museum in Preston.

SCOTLAND WON, ESTONIA DIDN'T TURN UP

The World Cup qualifier between Estonia and Scotland in 1996 had been scheduled to kick off in Talinn at 6.55 p.m. But when Scotland boss Craig Brown arrived at the ground he noticed the temporary floodlights were attached to the back of lorries and complained that they could dazzle his players. FIFA acted quickly and brought the kickoff forward to 3 p.m. This, however, did not impress the Estonian officials, who complained that not only would they be unable to get security staff in place so early but most of their own supporters would still be at work. As a result, when Scotland took to the field at 2.55 p.m., they were alone. Estonia had not turned up. Referee Miroslav Radoman dispensed with the coin-toss (in case Scotland's John Collins should call incorrectly), and duly blew his whistle to start the game. Billy Dodds passed the ball to Collins and then Radoman blew for full time as the Scottish fans chanted 'Easy, easy' from the terraces.

Unfortunately, FIFA then decided that instead of awarding Scotland the points, they would be forced to replay the match at a neutral venue. This time it wasn't so easy, as Brown's men struggled to a 0–0 draw in Monaco four months later.

THE WORST TEAM IN THE WORLD

In 1998 France proved they were the best team in the world by beating Brazil 3–0 in the World Cup final. But the worst team in the world had been decided long before that famous night in the Stade de France. In their six-match qualifying campaign in the Asian Zone, the Maldives lost 17–0 and 9–0 to Iran, 12–0 twice to Syria, and 6–0 and 3–0 to Kyrgyzstan. Their record of P6, L6, D0, F0 A59 remains the worst in World Cup history.

WIN OR DIE

Iraq needed to win their match against Kazakhstan in order to qualify for the 1998 World Cup. Disastrously, they lost 2–1. The president of the Iraqi FA was Uday Hussein, psychopathic son of Saddam, and a man who did not take defeat lightly. According to the testimony of two Iraqi players who have since defected to the West, several of the team were taken to the notorious Radwaniya prison, where they were shaved, dragged across gravel and then immersed in vats of raw sewage. The rest of the team were repeatedly beaten on the soles of their feet until they could hardly walk. FIFA sent a delegation to investigate the claims, but unsurprisingly they found only people who spoke in glowing terms about Uday and his methods.

DEATH OF A PRINCESS

The funeral of Princess Diana was scheduled for 6 September 1997. So was Scotland's World Cup qualifier against Belarus at Aberdeen. But while the rest of Britain closed down for the day, Jim Farry of the Scottish FA was determined that it should be business as usual. A huge row developed over whether playing the match would be disrespectful to the Princess's memory, with even the Scottish players at odds with each other. Gary McAllister said he was quite willing to play the game while striker Ally McCoist made it clear that if he was selected for a match on Saturday he would be forced to pull out. Eventually, after unseemly pressure was brought to bear, Farry conceded and the game was played the following day. The kerfuffle did not seem to affect the Scots unduly, as they ran out 4–1 winners.

ANTI-TERRORIST MEASURES

Such was the fear of terrorist attacks during the 2002 Japan/South Korea World Cup that extraordinary measures were put in place to ensure there would be no repetition of what had happened in New York the previous year. Anti-aircraft guns were installed inside the stadium at Seoul to prevent a terrorist spectacular during the opening match between France and Senegal, while a six-mile no-fly zone was installed around all the stadiums hosting matches. Meanwhile military forces in South Korea were put on a state of high alert and submarines and warships were deployed off the coast to thwart any maritime attacks.

WHAT MIGHT HAVE BEEN?

In March 1998 police and security forces raided a number of houses in Belgium and arrested seven members of an Algerian terror group. They subsequently discovered a chilling plot to create death and mayhem at that year's World Cup finals in France. First, the England team were to be massacred on the pitch using biological weapons. At the same time a group of armed terrorists would burst into the hotel used by the USA team and shoot them as they watched the match. The atrocity was planned as a dual attack on Britain and America and, although it failed, it meant that security at World Cups would from that moment on become a primary concern of FIFA.

TAKE-AWAY CURRY

In 1998, ten Scotland fans following their team in Bordeaux spent £600 on a take-away order of lager and curry which they telephoned through to the Eye of the Tiger restaurant in Bournemouth. They then spent a further £800 on a charter flight to deliver it to Bordeaux. Restaurant boss Mustafa Aolad said: 'It was such a good order we'd have liked to have delivered it free – but unfortunately it was beyond our usual five-mile radius. We all support Scotland now.'

ROMANIANS PREFER BLONDS

For their final group game against Tunisia at the Stade de France in 1998, the entire Romanian team dyed their hair peroxide blond – except for the goalkeeper, who was bald. 'This is a bonding exercise and a lucky charm to carry us all the way to the final,' explained coach Anghel Iordanescu. Fat lot of good it did them. After only managing to draw against Tunisia, the Romanians were sent packing in the knock-out stages by Croatia.

AUSSIES RUN RIOT

There have been many one-sided football games in World Cup history, but none to match the 31–0 drubbing handed out by Australia to little American Samoa at a qualifying match for the 2002 tournament. The first nine minutes were goalless, but then the floodgates opened. Goals were scored after 10, 12, 13, 14, 17, 19, 21, 23, 25, 27, 29, 32, 33, 37, 42 and 45 minutes. There then followed a 15-minute respite for half time before the slaughter continued with goals on 50, 51, 55, 56, 58, 60, 65, 66, 78, 80, 81, 84, 85, 88 and 89 minutes. Striker Archie Thompson's personal tally of 13 goals beat both the World Cup record (7) and Full International record (10) for a single game. 'We're here as a learning process,' said American Samoa manager Tony Langkilde. 'Our players' average age is 18. The only way is forward.'

SAN MARINO SHOCKER

San Marino, the tiny landlocked enclave in Northern Italy, is not renowned for its footballing prowess. Indeed most of the World Cup records they hold are for record defeats. Yet on 17 November 1993 the team of part-timers wrote themselves into the World Cup history books for all the right reasons: it's just unfortunate that their opponents that night were England. The game was a World Cup qualifier staged in nearby Bologna. England, under Graham Taylor, were as good as doomed to sit out the 1994 finals, but insult was very quickly added to injury when Stuart Pearce's underhit back-pass was pounced on by Davide Gualtieri, who hammered it into the net after just 8.3 seconds. Although the part-timers went on to lose 7–1, Gualtieri's goal was the quickest ever scored against England, and the fastest in a World Cup qualifier.

SEEING YELLOW AND RED

Welsh referee Clive Thomas was known as a stickler for the rules, but he was not a patch on Russian official Valentin Ivanov, who took charge of the 2006 World Cup clash between Portugal and Holland. During the course of the game Nieto showed a whopping sixteen yellow cards and four red cards – a record for a finals match, but perhaps par for the course in a tournament in which there were 345 yellows and 28 reds.

WHO US, REF?

Antonio Rattin may have got his marching orders during the stormy World Cup quarter-final between England and Argentina in 1966, but both Bobby and Jack Charlton were booked. However, because this was the last tournament before the introduction of red and yellow cards, neither brother realised until the following day.

THE 12TH MAN

Shortly before his team's World Cup match against Portugal in 2002, a South Korean fan in the city of Pusan committed suicide by dousing himself in paint thinner and setting himself alight. It was only later, when his suicide note was discovered, that his reasons became clear:

'I am choosing death because South Korea has far to go to compete with Latin American and European teams. So I will be a ghost, the 12th player on the pitch, and do my best for the team.'

Did he succeed? In 2002 South Korea confounded all the experts by reaching the semi-finals of the World Cup, where they were only narrowly pipped 1–0 by Germany.

SURPLUS TO REQUIREMENTS

Ahn Jung-Hwan missed what appeared to be a crucial penalty in South Korea's quarter-final match against Italy in 2002. But with the game stuck at 1–1 in extra time, the long-haired Ahn became an instant hero when he scored the winning 'Golden Goal' to put his side through to the semis. The Italians were not impressed, especially Luciano Gaucci, president of Ahn's Italian club Perugia, who immediately sacked the Korean. Gaucci claimed that it was not Ahn's goal which had annoyed him so much as his comments after the game. 'He said Korean football was superior to Italian football, when Italy is a footballing nation. We have treated him well with all our love, but his comments were offensive to me and the entire Italian nation.' Gaucci added: 'He was a phenomenon only when he played against Italy. I am a nationalist and I regard such behaviour not only as an affront to Italian pride but also an offence to a country which two years ago opened its doors to him. I have no intention of paying a salary to someone who has ruined Italian soccer.' However, Gaucci later changed his mind and reinstated Ahn to the squad after protests from his own supporters.

CAMEROON'S KIT

In 2002 Cameroon arrived in Japan and South Korea sporting a natty piece of kit: skin-tight, sleeveless shirts. Unfortunately for them, the stuffed shirts of FIFA's hierarchy ruled that because they didn't have sleeves they were vests – in contravention of the laws. Although Cameroon pointed out that they'd worn their vest shirts during the African Cup of Nations, FIFA were having none of it. Threatened with expulsion, Cameroon reluctantly obeyed and added sleeves to the ensemble.

LOTHAR'S RECORD

In attempting to clear the ball during a game against Mexico in 1998, Germany's Lothar Matthaus hit his own post and very nearly scored an own goal. Ironically, had the ball gone in it would have secured Matthaus a place in history as one of only three men to have scored in four successive World Cup tournaments. As it was, he would fail to score in 1998.

TIME DIFFERENCE

Due to the time difference between South Korea and California, in 2002 USA star striker Landon Donovan was able to play for his country in a losing World Cup quarter-final on Friday and for his team, San José, on Saturday.

RONALDO'S BAD-HAIR DAY

A major talking point of the 2002 semi-final between Brazil and Turkey was striker Ronaldo's bizarre hairstyle, which was shaved except for a prominent tuft at the front. It transpired that in a previous game, Ronaldo's son, Ronald, had thought his dad was defender Roberto Carlos. A quick once-over with the clippers left nobody in any doubt – although the little lad must have wished he'd kept his mouth shut.

WORST WORLD CUP

On the day of the 2002 World Cup final, the world's worst teams got together for a special match to celebrate their spectacular ordinariness. Montserrat, rated 203rd in the FIFA rankings, took a five-day trip to the Himalayan kingdom of Bhutan, rated 202nd. Bhutan won the game 4–0 in front of 15,000 fans – twice the population of Montserrat. Afterwards the two sides had a slap-up meal together and watched Brazil beat Germany on the TV.

DE BRITO'S HOWLER

Valdemar de Brito of Brazil became the first player to miss a penalty in a World Cup when he blazed wide during his team's 3–1 defeat against Italy in 1934. Another first of which de Brito was rather more proud was that he was the first scout to spot the potential of a young player called Edson Arantes de Nascimento – better known as Pelé.

WORLD CUP WILLIE

World Cup Willie, a lion-like character first unveiled in England in 1966, was the first ever World Cup mascot.

SHIRT SWAPPING

Although it dated back to 1954, the post-match practice of shirt-swapping was temporarily banned in 1986 because FIFA objected to the sight of bare chests on a football field.

GROUP OF DEATH

The term 'Group of Death' was first coined by the Mexican press in 1970 to describe Group 3, which consisted of England (reigning champions), Brazil (winners in 1958 and 1962), Czechoslovakia (finalists in 1962) and Romania.

1–0

1–0 is the most frequent score in World Cup matches.

COMMON NAME

The most common name in World Cup finals is Gonzales (or Gonzalez), which has featured fifteen times since 1930.

UNLUCKY LUXEMBOURG

Plucky Luxembourg have attempted – and failed – to qualify for every World Cup finals since 1934. They have participated in 92 qualifying matches, losing 88, scoring 45 goals and conceding 308. The only two teams they have ever beaten are Portugal (4–2 in 1961) and Turkey (2–0 in 1972).

SAN MARINO SUCCESS

San Marino's 1–0 win over Liechtenstein in a qualifying match for the 2006 World Cup in April 2004 was their first competitive win in 73 years.

WORLD CUP FIRSTS: MATCHES

- ⚽ **First match** Mexico 1, France 4 in Montevideo, Uruguay, 1930.
- ⚽ **First tied match** Italy 1, Spain 1 in Florence, Italy, 1934.
- ⚽ **First match with extra time** Austria vs France, 1934.
- ⚽ **First final with extra time** Italy vs Czechoslovakia, 1934.
- ⚽ **First scoreless match** Brazil vs England in Stockholm, Sweden, 1958.
- ⚽ **First match decided on penalty shoot-out** Semi-final between West Germany and France, 1982, in which the Germans won the shoot-out 5–4.
- ⚽ **First final decided on penalty shoot-out** The 1994 final in which Brazil beat Italy 3–2 after a 0–0 tie.
- ⚽ **First match played indoors** USA vs Switzerland at Pontiac Silverdome, Detroit, USA, 1994.
- ⚽ **First match in which a coach was sent off** Paraguayan coach Cayetano Re in a match against Belgium, 1986.

WORLD CUP FIRSTS: GOALS

- ⚽ **First goal in World Cup** Lucien Laurent of France against Mexico in the 19th minute in the first World Cup match, 1930.
- ⚽ **First penalty goal** Mexico's Manuel Rocquetas Rosas against Argentina, 1930.

⊛ **First penalty goal in a final** Johan Neeskens of Holland against West Germany, 1974.

⊛ **First hat trick** Guillermo Stabile of Argentina in their 6–3 win over Mexico, 1930.

⊛ **First extra-time goal** Austria's Anton Schall in the match against France, 1934.

⊛ **First first-minute goal** Emile Veinante of France in the 40th second of the match against Belgium, 1938.

⊛ **First own goal** Ernst Loertscher of Switzerland against West Germany, 1938.

⊛ **First goal by a substitute** Mexico's Juan Basaguren in the match against El Salvador, 1970.

⊛ **First hat trick by a substitute** Laszlo Kiss of Hungary in a match against El Salvador, 1982.

⊛ **First Golden Goal** France's Laurent Blanc in the 113th minute in the second-round match against Paraguay, 1998.

YOU AGAIN?

Throughout its often troubled history, FIFA have always been able to rely on Brazil to turn up for the World Cup. In fact they have played 87 matches over the seventeen tournaments since 1930, more than any other country. No wonder they've won it more than anybody else!

NOT JUST BRAZIL

Ask anyone which team has appeared in the most finals in the World Cup, and they will most probably say Brazil. But that would be to forget about Europe's most tenacious silverware hunters, Germany. In fact both nations have appeared in seven finals: Brazil in 1950, 1958, 1962, 1970, 1994, 1998, 2002 and Germany in 1954, 1966, 1974, 1982, 1986, 1990, 2002. Strangely, the 2002 final was the only one in which they appeared together.

BRAZIL WINNERS

Brazil have won 64 World Cup matches, more than any other nation. In 2002 they won seven on the trot, equalling the record held by Italy between 1934–8. Mexico, by contrast, hold the record for the most defeats with twenty. They have also lost the most consecutive matches, nine, between 1930 and 1958.

IMPREGNABLE ITALY

In 1990, Italy went five matches – or 450 minutes – without conceding a goal, which is a World Cup record. The run took them through to the semi-final where they survived a further 67 minutes intact before conceding to Claudio Caniggia of Argentina. That goal took the match into extra time and then penalties, in which Italy conceded four while only managing to convert three.

MARVELLOUS MATTHAUS AND MALDINI

Between 1982 and 1998 Germany's powerhouse midfielder Lothar Matthaus played an unrivalled 25 consecutive World Cup finals matches. During that time he won a winner's medal and a runner's up medal. However, the record for the most completed matches belongs to Italy's evergreen Paulo Maldini, who managed 23 without being substituted between 1990 and 2002.

EL CAPITANO MARADONA

A lesser-known record held by Argentina's Diego Maradona is that he captained his side sixteen times in World Cup matches.

AHEAD OF THE REST

Miroslav Klose of Germany scored five goals with his head during World Cup 2002 in Japan/South Korea, the most by any player in finals history.

SHILTS RECORD

England's goalkeeper Peter Shilton kept a record ten clean sheets in World Cup matches between 1982 and 1990. In 1982 he conceded just one, in 1986 he was beaten three times, and in 1990 he let in four – if you don't count the four West Germany scored in the penalty shoot-out. Eight goals in three World Cup tournaments – and England never went further than the semis.

STILL THE BOSS

While most countries are happy to give their coach at least one tilt at the World Cup before sacking him, Germany clearly believe that managerial consistency is the key to success. And who can argue? Between 1966 and 1978 Helmut Schoen led his side to four World Cups, two World Cup finals and one World Cup final victory.

SPOT-KICK KINGS

It always pays to have a top-notch penalty taker on your side. Four of Eusebio's nine goals in the 1966 World Cup were from the spot, a record equalled only by Robbie Rensenbrink of Holland in 1978.

COMEDY OF ERRORS

The USA's 3–2 win over Portugal in the 2002 finals was one of the big shocks in a competition in which the minnows generally acquitted themselves well. It was also the first time in World Cup history that a match featured two own goals. Already trailing by a fourth-minute goal, Portugal made life even more difficult for themselves when Jorge Costa put one into his own net on 29 minutes. Leading 3–1 in the second half and seemingly cruising to victory, Jeff Agoos duly beat his own keeper to set up a nerve-wracking last twenty minutes for the Americans.

KOREAN NIGHTMARE

Pity poor Yung Hong Duk. As the last line of a largely non-existent South Korean defence, the goalkeeper was always going to be in for a torrid time at the 1954 World Cup. And so it proved. In just two matches he picked the ball out of his own net a record sixteen times as his side collapsed 9–0 to Hungary and 7–0 to Turkey.

GOALS, GOALS, GOALS

At times there have been questions about their defence, but Brazil's philosophy has always been that it doesn't matter how many they score, as long as we score more. Reckless, perhaps – but with 201 goals between 1930 and 2002, the South Americans are by far the most prodigious finishers in World Cup history.

NUMBERS UP

The 1938 finals in France was the first time numbers were used on players' shirts in the World Cup.

GERMAN EFFICIENCY?

They are renowned for their defensive qualities and, in Franz Beckenbauer, possessed perhaps the World Cup's most complete defender. Yet amazingly Germany (and West Germany) have conceded 112 goals in their World Cup finals appearances – more than any other country. Fourteen of those goals were conceded over six matches in 1954, the year they first won the Jules Rimet trophy. Mind you, Germany have played more matches than anyone else apart from Brazil.

Viva World Cup!

ALLEZ LES BLEUS AND MODERN CATENACCIO

In winning the World Cup on home turf in 1998, France conceded just two goals – at that time, the fewest by any World Cup-winning side. This record was subsequently equalled by a similarly mean-spirited Italian defence, led by FIFA World Player of the Year Fabio Cannavaro, during the 2006 World Cup.

RED AND YELLOW CARDS

Peru's captain Mario de Las Casas became the first player to be sent off in World Cup history when he was given his marching orders in a match against Romania in 1930. However, the first player to receive the red card was Chile's Carlos Caszely in a match against West Germany 44 years later. The first yellow card had been shown to Evgeny Lovchev of the USSR in 1970, again against West Germany.

THE SCORPION STUNG

Following in a long tradition of lunatic South American goalkeepers, Colombia's Rene Higuita earned himself a place in the history books in 1990 when, for reasons better known to himself, he decided to dribble the ball all the way from his own penalty area to the halfway line. As his teammates watched open-mouthed, Higuita was duly dispossessed by Cameroon's Roger Milla, who gleefully ran off and scored.

BORN WINNERS

The only European players to have won two World Cups are Italy's Giuseppe Meazza and Giovanni Ferrari, who both played in the 1934 and 1938 champion teams. Meanwhile the only player to have won an impressive three World Cups is the peerless Pelé of Brazil, who gained winners medals in 1958, 1962 and 1970.

176

BROTHERS WHO HAVE PLAYED IN WORLD CUP FINALS

⚽ Juan and Marino Evaristo of Argentina (1930)
⚽ Fritz and Ottmar Walter of West Germany (1954)
⚽ Jack and Bobby Charlton of England (1966)
⚽ René and Willy van der Kerkhof of Holland (1978)

OTHER SIGNIFICANT EVENTS IN WORLD CUP YEARS

1930 First Empire Games held in Hamilton; Vannevar Bush and a team of scientists develop the 'Differential Analyzer', arguably first modern computer; planet Pluto discovered (now recategorized as a dwarf planet).

1934 Austrian Nazis murder Austrian Chancellor Dollfuss; Adolf Hitler combines positions of Chancellor and President and becomes 'Führer' of Germany; 'Night of the Long Knives'.

1938 Civil War in Spain ends; German troops invade Austria; Orson Welles' broadcast of *War of the Worlds* causes panic across the USA; Lázló Bíró invents the ballpoint pen.

1950 Korean War begins; Florence Chadwick swims the Channel in 13 hours 22 minutes; comic strip Peanuts is published in the USA, featuring Good Ol' Charlie Brown; Shirley Temple retires from showbiz.

1954 *Fellowship of the Ring* is published, beginning the *Lord of the Rings* trilogy; Brown vs Board of Education of Topeka goes before the Supreme Court, resulting in the end of racial segregation; Roger Bannister runs the four-minute mile; *Playboy* is first published.

1958 The Treaty of Rome marks the foundation of the European Economic Community; the Munich air disaster kills 21, including seven Manchester

United players; Nikita Khrushchev becomes Soviet premier; the first parking meters are introduced in the UK.

1962 John Glen becomes the first American to orbit the Earth; the Rolling Stones make their debut in London; the Cuban missile crisis brings the world to the brink of war; the Big Freeze hits the UK, with sub-zero temperatures until March 1963.

1966 Indira Ghandi of India becomes the first woman Prime Minister; John Lennon claims the Beatles are 'more popular than Jesus'; the first episode of Star Trek is aired; a landslide in Aberfan, Wales, kills dozens of schoolchildren.

1970 Four students are shot dead by guardsmen at Kent State University; the Beatles split; Jimi Hendrix dies of a drugs overdose; General de Gaulle of France dies.

1974 President Nixon resigns due to his involvement in the Watergate scandal; a kidnap attempt on Princess Anne in the Mall fails; Lord Lucan disappears.

1978 The film *Grease* is released; Louise Brown, the first test-tube baby, is born; Bishop Karol Wojtyla of Poland becomes Pope John Paul II; the People's Republic of China lifts its ban on Shakespeare and Charles Dickens.

1982 The Falklands War breaks out; Kielder Water, a man-made lake, opens in Northumberland; Michael Fagan breaks into the Queen's bedroom; King Henry VIII's flagship *Mary Rose* is raised from the Solent after 400 years.

1986 The space shuttle Challenger explodes; Swedish prime minister Olaf Palme is shot dead; Prince Andrew marries Sarah Ferguson; fire breaks out at the Chernobyl nuclear reactor in the Ukraine.

1990 McDonald's opens a branch in Moscow; Nelson Mandela is released from captivity in South Africa; poll tax riots break out in London; the first Gulf War breaks out when US and coalition forces invade Iraq.

1994 The Church of England ordains its first women priests; ice skater Tonya Harding is convicted of organising an attack on her rival Nancy Kerrigan; Nirvana singer Kurt Cobain shoots himself; racing driver Ayrton Senna is killed.

1998 US President Bill Clinton is embroiled in the Monica Lewinsky sex scandal; Dana International, a transsexual from Israel, wins the Eurovision song contest; Internet search engine Google is started.

2002 US troops invade Afghanistan; the Queen Mother dies; the Queen celebrates her Golden Jubilee.

2006 The first case of bird flu is discovered in the UK; Lordi win the Eurovision Song Contest; Al Qaeda leader Abu Musab al-Zarqari is killed in Iraq; Google buys YouTube for $1.65 billion.

2010 The Deepwater Horizon oil rig explodes in the Mexican Gulf; the Eyjafjallajökull volcano erupts in Iceland, causing global air-traffic disruption; 33 Chilean miners are freed after 69 days trapped underground; an earthquake causes widespread death and destruction in Haiti.

VOODOO CHILD

Before the 1974 tournament in West Germany, Haiti revealed their secret weapon for World Cup success: voodoo. However, the use of a witch doctor didn't appear to help their cause, as they lost 3–1 to Italy, 7–0 to Poland and then 4–1 to Argentina.

HAITI

Knowing that Papa Doc Duvalier was watching from the stands and understandably fearing for his safety should the home side lose, the referee in the World Cup qualifier between Haiti and visitors Trinidad contrived to disallow four perfectly good Trinidad goals as Haiti went on to win 2–1 and qualify for the 1974 finals in West Germany.

THE FIRST WORLD CHAMPIONS?

After beating English FA Cup winners West Bromwich Albion 4–1 at Hampden Park, Glasgow in a friendly match in 1888 – nearly 30 years before the first World Cup in Uruguay – Scottish Cup winners Renton declared themselves 'Champions of the United Kingdom and the World' and even had a trophy made to reinforce the fact. Such success did not last long, however. The following season the World Champions fell into financial difficulty and were forced to drop out of the league.

CAFÉ CULTURE

Belgium's star player Raymond Braine was suspended from the whole of the 1930 tournament – by his own football association. His crime? Opening a café!

WEST AUCKLAND WIN THE WORLD CUP

In 1909 tea magnate Sir Thomas Lipton decided to organise a 'world football tournament' to be held in Turin, Italy. But when he approached the FA about sending a team, they refused. Undeterred, Lipton chose West Auckland Town, a team consisting mostly of miners that was languishing third from bottom of the Northern Amateur League (it is thought one of the main reasons for choosing them was because their initials, WAFC, were the same as Woolwich Arsenal). Having sold most of their possessions to finance their trip, West

Auckland not only took part in the four-team competition, but won it, beating Stuttgarter Sportfreund of Germany and FC Winterthur of Switzerland in the final to lift the 'Crown of Italy World Cup'. Not only that, but two years later the lads from County Durham did it again, this time beating the mighty Juventus 6–1 in the final. For this they were allowed to keep the trophy in perpetuity, and it remained behind the bar of West Auckland social club until 1994 when, like all good World Cup trophies, it was stolen.

NORTH KOREA NOT WELCOME

English fans took the North Koreans to their hearts in 1966 – but not the British government. Documents released 30 years later revealed how the prospect of communists on English soil filled the Foreign Office with dread. Among the secret moves to get them kicked out of the tournament were denying them entrance visas to the UK. When this didn't work, a plan was put into force designed to 'minimise the visual presence' and 'avoid doing anything where possible which might imply a diplomatic acceptance of the regime'. This included insisting that the team play as 'North Korea' and not the Democratic People's Republic of Korea, not inviting them to the World Cup draw, restricting Royal attendance to their matches and, unusually, banning the playing of national anthems except at the opening ceremony and the final. The North Koreans were also despatched to Middlesbrough and Liverpool to play their matches – a move that backfired spectacularly when the natives decided that the spirit of football was far more important than Cold War politicking.

POLICE ASSISTANCE

In the 1930 semi-final between Uruguay and Yugoslavia, the host's third goal in their 6–1 rout was scored after the ball ran out of play – and was neatly sidefooted back on by a uniformed policeman patrolling the touchline. All of the officials pretended not to notice, but then again the referee was Brazilian Gilberto Rega, who had already made a name for himself by ending the France vs Argentina match six minutes early by mistake.

ITALY QUALIFY

In 1934 FIFA decided that in the interests of fairness, even the nominated host country, Italy, should have to qualify for the finals. It seems not to have occurred to them what might have happened if the Italians had lost their vital playoff against Greece. Fortunately the Italians were not prepared to let that happen. After beating Greece 4–0 in Milan, they successfully 'persuaded' their opponents that the second leg was not necessary. To do this, the Italians funded and built a new headquarters for the Greek FA in Athens on the understanding that they would concede the game.

THE SAAR

Having spent most of its existence being passed between neighbours France and Germany, in 1953 the tiny principality known as The Saar was enjoying one of its rare periods of independence. To celebrate this, they applied to take part in the 1954 World Cup finals and were duly entered into a qualifying group which included Norway and West Germany. Amazingly, The Saar beat Norway 3–2 – but their dreams of performing on the World Cup stage were destroyed by the Germans who not only beat them but later rubbed salt into the wound by reassimilating them.

BLIND BALLOT

FIFA's intransigence about its rules reached farcical proportions in 1954 when, despite a 4–2 lead on aggregate over two legs, Spain were forced to play a decider against Turkey on neutral ground in Rome's Olympic Stadium for the right to reach the finals themselves. When this match finished 2–2, it was

decided to draw lots to see who would go through. In order to ratchet up the
tension a fourteen-year-old boy called Luigi Franco Gemma was brought out
onto the pitch, blindfolded, and in front of a 40,000 crowd, asked to select
one name from a large drum. Almost inevitably the name he selected was
Turkey – which meant that despite winning 6–4 on aggregate, Spain were
eliminated from the 1954 World Cup.

ROMARIO LOTHARIO

Brazil striker Romario claimed that during the 1994 World Cup he slept with
no fewer than three women a day.

SUN TRAP

After 23 minutes of their 1954 quarter-final tie against Austria in Lausanne,
hosts Switzerland were cruising at 3–0. Yet by half time the Austrians had
staged a remarkable recovery to lead 5–4. Perhaps embarrassed by the ease
and swiftness with which the Austrians had regained the initiative, the Swiss
officials came up with a novel excuse. A hastily drafted release was circulated
in the press box claiming that 'All goals scored against Switzerland owing to
the sun'. The sun did not bother the Austrians in the second half, as they added
two more goals to run out convincing 7–5 winners.

DUCK, PAL

Sometimes those training-ground moves work out a treat. Such was the case
in 1974, when the below-par Brazil team nevertheless produced a moment
of magic against East Germany. Awarded a free kick on the edge of the box,
Jairzinho carefully took up position in the German wall. Up stepped Rivelino,
whose powerful shot was aimed directly at his teammate. On cue Jairzinho
ducked and the ball flew into the back of the net.

CRICKET STARS

West Indian cricket legend Viv Richards played for Antigua and Barbuda in their 1974 World Cup qualifying campaign. Meanwhile umpire Steve Bucknor started his officiating career as a football referee. In 1988 he took charge of the 1990 qualifying match between El Salvador and Netherlands Antilles. It was his only match at that level, as at the age of 45 he was obliged to stand down by FIFA. He went on to umpire in four cricket World Cup finals.

ZAIRE HOWLER

A 9–0 hammering at the hands of Yugoslavia in their group match in 1974 suggested that Zaire were one of the World Cup's more hopeless competitors. In their next match against Brazil, the Africans revealed that they knew as much about the laws of the game as they did about defending. Brazil were awarded a free kick on the edge of the box, but before Rivelino could take it, Zaire defender Mwepu sprinted from the wall and booted the ball away. Booked for his trouble, Mwepu explained later that he had seen other teams do it.

FLUMMOXED

At first it seemed that Scotland's World Cup woes had reached farcical proportions, but when Graeme Souness and Frank Gray appeared to run into each other as the Scots prepared to take a free kick against New Zealand in their opening group match of the 1982 finals, laughter turned to roars of appreciation as John Robertson used the clever diversion to curl the dead ball into the back of the net past a distracted defence.

RED FACE FOR YELLOW CARD POLL

Referee Graham Poll was selected to officiate at the 2006 finals because, allegedly, he was the top whistleblower in England. His World Cup pedigree was decidedly patchy, however. In 2002 he disallowed two perfectly good

Italian goals during a 2–1 defeat to Croatia – and four years later, he very nearly did the Croatians another favour in their crunch Group F clash against Australia. Defender Josip Šimunic had already been booked once when he committed another blatant foul. Poll duly reached for his pocket – and produced another yellow. Despite the error being pointed out in no uncertain terms by the Socceroos, Poll, who had already sent off two players, maintained he was right. Four minutes later, when Šimunic committed yet another bookable offence, he was duly given a red card. The match finished 2–2, and the Aussies managed to scrape through to the knockout stage. But it was too late for the hapless Poll, who was himself booked – onto the next plane home.

MARADONA ON THE SLIDE

As a player Diego Maradona scored some pretty crucial World Cup goals for Argentina. But arguably the most important goal in the Albiceleste's illustrious history was scored with Maradona as manager. After a wretched qualifying campaign for the 2010 finals, Argentina found themselves needing to beat Peru in their penultimate match to at least give them a chance of going through by beating Uruguay in the final group game. They duly took the lead, but when Peru equalised in the 90th minute it seemed the unthinkable was about to come true. Then, in the third minute of stoppage time, veteran midfielder Martin Palermo was in the right place to fire home a dramatic winner. Maradona, famous for his energetic goal celebrations as a player, surpassed himself by joyfully sliding fully twenty yards along the touchline.

THE HAND OF HENRY

Thirteen years after Maradona's infamous 'Hand of God' goal against England, the World Cup was rocked by yet another incident of blatant handball. This time the victims were the Republic of Ireland, who were playing France in a nerve-jangling playoff for the 2010 finals. With the scores level at 1–1 in extra time, and the match in Paris heading for penalties, the ball squirted through to

Thierry Henry on the byline. Henry, renowned as one of the finest and fairest players ever to grace a football pitch, clearly used his hand to control the ball not once but twice before squaring for William Gallas to blast home the winner. Neither referee Martin Hansson nor his assistants saw the incident – and despite everybody in the stadium seeing the foul on the big screen replays, the goal stood and the Irish were out.

JOSÉ PEKS THE WRONG MAN

When Argentina destroyed Serbia and Montenegro 6–0 in a scintillating display of attacking football during the 2006 group stages, it seemed we were not only watching the World Champions elect but, in young Lionel Messi, a worthy successor to the great Diego Maradona. But we all reckoned without the aptly named Argentine coach José Pekerman, who pretty much single-handedly scuppered his own team's chances in the quarter-final against Germany by leaving the brilliant Messi on the bench and substituting his other star player, Juan Riquelme, with the score just 1–0 to the South Americans. The Germans duly equalised and then, as usual, went on to win on penalties. Stunned, the Argentines kicked off a mini riot on the pitch, with players and officials joining in the sorry free-for-all.

GOODBYE TO ALL THAT

Seventy years after it hosted the 1936 Olympic Games, the Olympiastadion in Berlin was the natural choice as venue for the 2006 World Cup Final. It was here, of course, that Adolf Hitler saw the great Jesse Owens win four gold medals – and its historic significance was not lost on the architects responsible for redesigning it at a cost of €242 million. In particular the iconic stone towers at the entrance remained a focal point, despite many Germans wanting the whole structure torn down. According to Interior Minister Otto Schily, the stadium recalled 'all the dark elements present in its creation. But in 2006 the world will look upon to modern, democratic, and open Germany.'

GREAT GAMES: ARGENTINA 2–1 MEXICO, 2006

In a tournament sorely lacking in quality, goals or indeed excitement, this all-South American second-round clash had it all.

Argentina, with the likes of Riquelme, Crespo, Tevez and the mercurial 18-year-old Lionel Messi in the squad, were the red-hot favourites to progress to the quarter finals, having played with joyous abandon and deadly intent during the group stage. Mexico, meanwhile, had stuttered through with a string of unimpressive performances against weak opposition.

A crowd of 43,000 in Leipzig sat back to watch the inevitable slaughter – but the Mexicans were determined they were not there to make up the numbers. Rocked by a series of pulsating attacks, the Argentines were floored after just eight minutes when, from a wide free kick, Rafael Marquez stole in at the back post to smash the ball into the roof of the net.

Normal service appeared to have been resumed five minutes later when Mexico's Borghetti bundled a corner into his own net to level the scores. But despite thrills, spills and chances galore at both ends, the match was still tied after 90 minutes – and it would take a goal of stunning quality to settle matters.

It came eight minutes into extra time when Argentina's Maxi Rodriguez, controlling an innocuous-looking ball on the corner of the Mexico penalty area, volleyed an absolute peach into the far corner of the net. It was one of the goals of the tournament, and a fitting way to decide its best game.

GOALS OF THE TOURNAMENT 2010

It was not a vintage World Cup by any stretch of the imagination, yet the 2010 tournament nevertheless produced a number of stunning goals. These were the best 10, as chosen by subscribers to FIFA.com.

GABRIEL HEINZE, for Argentina against Nigeria The Manchester United fullback appears from nowhere to meet Veron's pin-point corner with a diving header which flies into the top corner of the net from 10 yards.

SULLEY MUNTARI, for Ghana against Uruguay It's first-half injury time in a tight quarter-final, Muntari picks up the ball 40 yards out and unleashes an unstoppable left-foot shot that briefly raises the possibility that Ghana could be on their way to a historic semi-final berth.

LUCAS PODOLSKI, for Germany against England Shell-shocked England are ripped to shreds by Germany in this quarter-final tie, and Podolski's exquisite finish from an acute angle following a devastating counterattack is the pick of the Germans' four goals.

FABIO QUAGLIARELLA, for Italy against Slovakia A desperately disappointing Italy are already trailing 3–1 and heading out of the World Cup in the group stages when Quagliarella's last-gasp precision chip from 30 yards salvages a little respect.

SIPHIWE TSHABALALA for South Africa against Mexico Not simply a historic goal but a belter in its own right as Tshabalala latches on to a defence-splitting through ball and smashes a left-foot beauty into the top corner of the Mexican net.

LUIS SUAREZ for Uruguay against Mexico A moment of genius from the diminutive striker, who receives the ball wide on the left and surrounded by defenders, yet is able to jink inside and curl a beautiful right-foot shot around the keeper into the far corner.

CARLOS TEVEZ for Argentina against Mexico The luckless Mexicans are once again the victims of some sublime skill as Tevez beats two defenders on the edge of the box before striking a fearsome drive into the net from 25 yards.

MESUT OZIL for Germany against Ghana A tense group game is decided by wunderkind Ozil's spectacular half-volley from 25 yards after some typically crisp German build-up play.

GIOVANNI VAN BRONCKHORST for Holland against Uruguay A goal out of nothing from the Dutch skipper, who darts down the left flank and then amazes everyone by smashing a brilliant shot into the opposite corner of the net.

DIEGO FORLAN for Uruguay against Germany A goal befitting the tournament's best player in a third-place playoff that would have made a brilliant final. Forlan's athletic volley from the edge of the box is perfectly executed to leave the German keeper standing.

HOT-SHOT HIT LIST

Here's a list of the bookies' favourites to top the scoring charts in Brazil:

Cristiano Ronaldo (Portugal) Considered by many to be at the peak of his powers, Ronaldo has been scoring for fun for Real Madrid and could prove devastating if he can receive the necessary support from his teammates.

Lionel Messi (Argentina) Could this be the Messi World Cup? If his extraordinary form for Barcelona over the last four years is anything to go by then the diminutive genius could be about to etch his name in history.

Neymar (Brazil) It's been a while since we've had a Brazilian to purr over, but at 22 the brilliant Neymar will have his home World Cup as a stage to parade his lethal goalscoring prowess.

Franck Ribery (France) One of the few players to emerge with any credit from the French debacle in 2010, Ribery will be hoping for solidarity in the ranks this time round. On his day a world-beater.

Mesut Ozil (Germany) After making a name for himself in South Africa, Ozil is now at the heart of a powerful German side that has evolved around their Arsenal playmaker. A scorer and creator of goals.

Luis Suarez (Uruguay) After a transcendent season with Liverpool, Uruguay will be looking to Suarez to propel them one step further than 2014's semi-final place.

Thomas Muller (Germany) The prolific German goalscorer won the Golden Boot in South Africa, and there is nothing to suggest he has lost any of his predatory instincts in front of goal.

Andres Iniesta (Spain) One of the prime architects at the heart of the Spanish midfield, Iniesta's goal won the World Cup in 2010. But is this a tournament too far for the tiki-taka magicians?

Isco (Spain) Francisco Roman Alarcon Suarez, aka Isco, has been a star for the Spanish junior sides. Now he has the chance to make a name for himself on the biggest stage of all.

Robinho (Brazil) After a disappointing spell at Manchester City, Robinho's career was revitalised by a move back to Brazil and a subsequent transfer to Milan. But will he be weighed down by the hopes of the Brazilian nation?

Sergio Aguero (Argentina) Another South American who has thrived in England, Aguero will be looking to link up with Lionel Messi at the spearhead of a lethal Argentine front line.

RONALDO'S A WINKER

England's stuttering 2006 World Cup campaign came to a merciful end when Portugal beat them on penalties following a fractious goalless draw in Gelsenkirchen. Apart from yet another shoot-out calamity for England, the game was marked by the sending off of the frustrated Wayne Rooney for appearing to stamp on Ricardo Carvalho. As Rooney tramped from the pitch, his Manchester United teammate Cristiano Ronaldo was seen to wink knowingly at the Portuguese bench – suggesting that not only was getting under the England player's skin a tactic, but that it had succeeded perfectly.

RED-CARD ARGIE

The referee who sent off Wayne Rooney was the Argentine Horacio Elizondo. Eight days later he would wave a red at Zinedine Zidane for his headbutt on Marco Materazzi in the World Cup Final.

HAT TRICK OF SHAME

Wayne Rooney's sending off against Portugal made him the third English player to receive his marching orders during a World Cup match. He joined Ray Wilkins (1986) and David Beckham (1998) who also saw a direct red card in a World Cup encounter; the former for throwing the ball at the referee during a group game vs. Morocco, and the latter for petulantly kicking out at Argentinian midfielder Diego Simeone.

BIG PHIL'S INDIAN SIGN

England's defeat by Portugal meant they had been eliminated by a Luiz Felipe Scolari-led side in the last three major tournaments (Brazil, 2002; Portugal in 2004 and 2006, both on penalties).

SPORT FOR ALL

In 1936, the Olympics were broadcast across Berlin on 25 screens in selected venues across the city, the first time a major sporting event had ever been televised live. In 2006 fans who couldn't get a ticket for the Olympiastadion were able to enjoy the action on a 100 sq metre (1,000 sq ft) screen in a 20,000 capacity open-air amphitheatre just outside the ground.

BACK OF THE NETZER!

Former West German midfielder Günter Netzer was a 1970s legend who went on to become an equally popular TV pundit. During the 2006 semi-final between France and Portugal in Munich, he proved he had lost none of his old skills when the ball was kicked towards his commentary position. Netzer calmly stood and headed the ball back onto the pitch, then turned to fellow pundits Marcel Desailly and Leonardo and said, 'I've always wanted to do that.'

PENALTY PUT-OFF

There can be fewer more nerve-racking moments in a player's career than taking a penalty in the World Cup finals. Pity Sweden's Henrik Larsson, then, who was just about to take a vital spot kick against Germany in the opening match of the 2006 tournament, when his manager Lars Lagerbäck decided to make a substitution. His concentration shot, Larsson fluffed the kick. Sweden duly lost the match 2–0.

A WORD FROM OUR SPONSORS

The 2006 tournament was the most commercial yet in terms of sponsorship from major global brands. But things reached a surreal stage when Dutch fans were told to remove their trousers if they wanted to watch the match against Argentina for fear of offending one of the big companies. More than 1,000 fans sporting orange lederhosen supplied by Dutch brewer Bavaria had to sit in their underpants on the orders of official sponsor Anheuser Busch, manufacturer of rival Budweiser beer.

DOCTOR ON CALL

Prior to the 2006 tournament Ecuador were taking no chances, and flew a witch doctor named Tzamaranda Nychapi to Germany in order to purify the stadiums where the South American side would be playing. Was it any coincidence that they unexpectedly progressed to the second round, where they were narrowly beaten by England?

HAIR TONIC

Prior to his team's game against Switzerland in 2006, Brazil star Ronaldinho donated two locks of his hair for an auction organised by a Swiss newspaper to raise money for a cancer charity.

LEADING LEAGUES

Leagues with the most players in the 2010 World Cup:
- ⚽ England 117
- ⚽ Germany 84
- ⚽ Italy 80
- ⚽ Spain 59
- ⚽ France 46

TOP TEN OR MORE

Here's a rundown of the clubs who had ten or more players in World Cup squads in 2010:
- ⚽ Chelsea 16
- ⚽ Barcelona 14
- ⚽ Arsenal 12
- ⚽ Aston Villa 12
- ⚽ Inter Milan 11
- ⚽ Bayern Munich 11
- ⚽ Real Madrid 11
- ⚽ Tottenham 10

BARMY UZBEKS

The award for shooting yourself in the foot goes to Uzbekistan, who, during a 2005 Asian group qualifying game against Bahrain, were awarded a penalty and duly scored it – despite a number of Bahrain players straying into the box. For some reason, however, they were incensed that Japanese referee Toshimitsu Yoshida had refused to order the spot kick to be retaken, even though the goal had earned the Uzbeks a 1–0 win. The matter was referred to FIFA, who took the unusual step of ordering the match to be replayed. Bahrain gleefully won the match, and Uzbekistan were eliminated from the tournament.

TOGO OR NOT TO GO

It was once the case that playing in the World Cup finals was the pinnacle of any player's career, one that they would do for free if asked. Not so with the players of Togo, who demanded 155,000 euros each to appear in Germany in 2006. When the Togolese FA told them to get lost, the players announced they were going on strike. This was all too much for manager Otto Pfister, who quit in disgust having managed to get the team to their first ever finals. He returned when the dispute was finally resolved on the eve of the tournament — and watched his team of overpaid superstars lose all three group games.

A MISS THAT LED TO A HIT?

There have been many explanations for Zinedine Zidane's crazy head-butt on Italy's Marco Materazzi in the 110th minute of the 2006 Final. Some commentators believe it has a lot to do with the French maestro's bullet header six minutes earlier that was amazingly tipped over the bar by Gianluigi Buffon. Not only would the goal have surely won the World Cup for France, it would have been the most career goals scored by a player in a World Cup final (four: two in the 1998 final against Brazil and France's opening goal in this match), and the most scored by a captain (two). In the event he did claim one record — the first player to be sent off in extra time of a World Cup final. Zidane held this dubious distinction until it was matched by John Heitinga, who was dismissed in the 109th minute of the 2010 final.

ON THE MONEY

In 2008, journalist Declan Hill claimed that four 2006 World Cup Finals matches were fixed by a betting syndicate based in Bangkok. Among the matches allegedly affected were those between Ghana and Italy in the group stages, Ghana and Brazil in the round of 16, and Ukraine and Italy in the quarter-final. Stephen Appiah, the Ghana captain, later confirmed that he had been targeted by match-fixers, although team bosses have denied the allegations.

HANDY MILAN

There is no doubting the handiest player at the 2006 World Cup. Serbia and Montenegro's Milan Dudic deliberately handled the ball in the box on two occasions during his team's match against the Ivory Coast. As a result he was sent off, Ivory Coast scored both penalties, and Serbia and Montenegro lost the match 3–2.

POISON PEN FOR SVEN

Blame for England's lamentable performance at the 2006 World Cup was laid firmly at the door of manager Sven-Göran Eriksson – at least by members of the press, who were nothing less than scathing in their verdict of the Swede's stewardship. 'We've sold our birthright down the fjord to a nation of seven million skiers and hammer throwers who spend half their lives in darkness,' said Daily Mail hack Jeff Powell.

And there were more vitriolic hacks queueing up to pour scorn on poor Sven: 'This is the man who turned the golden generation into base metal, whose bedroom formations were far more adventurous than his footballing ones, who took us all for a ride but never had any idea where he was going,' said Martin Lipton of the Daily Mirror, while Brian Woolnough in the *Daily Star* said 'Sven-Göran Eriksson has been a £25m waste of money. An international fraud.'

ONLY HERE FOR THE BEER

Despite the distance and the expense, more than 25,000 England fans made the trip to South Africa in 2010. And as the team struggled on the pitch, it seemed the travelling army were concerned only with making the most of the hospitality before it was time to go home. In Rustenburg, a mining town in South Africa's North West Province where England were due to play the USA, organisers erected the biggest beer tent on the continent on a school playing field, while local bar owners ordered in an extra 1.2 million pints of lager to cope with the huge demand. When the red-and-white army marched on Port Elizabeth for the final group game, many of the bars were forced to close early after running out of beer. And within hours of the last-16 knockout tie against Germany being announced in Bloemfontein every room within 20 miles and all flights in and out of the city of Bloemfontein were sold out.

NOT BAD FOR A FAT LAD

The 2006 tournament was Brazil striker Ronaldo's fourth. Despite rumours that he was past his best, he still managed become the tournament's all-time highest scorer, scoring three to reach a total of 15 and surpassing West German Gerd Müller's long-standing record of 14.

POSTCARD FROM HOME

All 23 players in the Ivory Coast squad in 2006 were foreign-based. Indeed, only one player, the goalkeeper Jean-Jacques Tizie, played his club football outside Europe. The individual players' respective teams at the time were as follows:

1	GK	Jean-Jacques Tizie	(Esperance, TUN)
2	MF	Kanga Akale	(Auxerre, FRA)
3	DF	Arthur Boka	(Strasbourg, FRA)
4	DF	Kolo Toure	(Arsenal, ENG)
5	MF	Didier Zokora	(Saint-Etienne, FRA)
6	DF	Blaise Kouassi	(Troyes, FRA)
7	MF	Emerse Fae	(Nantes, FRA)
8	FW	Bonaventure Kalou	(Paris St-Germain, FRA)
9	FW	Arouna Kone	(PSV Eindhoven, NED)
10	MF	Gilles Yapi Yapo	(Young Boys, SUI)
11	FW	Didier Drogba	(Chelsea, ENG)
12	DF	Abdoulaye Meite	(Marseille, FRA)

13	DF	Marc Zoro	(Messina, ITA)
14	FW	Bakary Kone	(Nice, FRA)
15	FW	Aruna Dindane	(Lens, FRA)
16	GK	Gerard Gnanhouan	(Montpellier, FRA)
17	DF	Cyrille Domoraud	(Creteil, FRA)
18	MF	Kader Keita	(Lille, FRA)
19	MF	Yaya Toure	(Olympiakos, GRE)
20	MF	Guy Demel	(Hamburger SV, GER)
21	DF	Emmanuel Eboue	(Arsenal, ENG)
22	MF	Romaric	(Le Mans, FRA)
23	GK	Boubacar Barry	(Beveren, BEL)

SUN PUTS ROOF TECHNOLOGY IN THE SHADE

The German football authorities were understandably proud of the retractable roofs over their World Cup stadiums at Frankfurt and Gelsenkirchen. However, bright sunshine streaming onto the pitches was not everyone's cup of tea. TV broadcasters in particular were peeved that the inevitable shadows late in the game were proving annoying to their viewers and suggested that the stadium roofs should be shut. FIFA, thankfully, took the players' best interests at heart for once and decided a few shadows were a less distressing sight than 22 footballers suffocating in the heat.

TYROS AND OLDIES

The youngest squad at the 2010 World Cup was Ghana, with an average age of 24.1 years. The oldest was England (28.7). Tournament winners Spain had one of the youngest squads, with an average age of 25.9.

EUROPEAN CUP

The 2006 tournament was the first World Cup with three Portuguese-speaking national football teams, namely Portugal, Brazil and Angola. It also featured the first all-European semi-finals since the finals of 1982.

WHAT'S IN A NAME?

Such is the power of the World Cup sponsors, FIFA will do anything to ensure they get things their way. That includes riding roughshod over any existing sponsorship deals the host country might have arranged. In Germany, this even included renaming stadiums in case they should offend the moneymen. For example the Allianz Arena in Munich was reinvented as the FIFA World Cup Stadium, Munich for the duration of the tournament, and any company logo or mention of the Allianz firm was carefully erased from the ground as well as its surroundings.

TEAM GAME

No player from the winning Italian squad scored more than two goals during the 2006 tournament – though ten different players had scored for the team, tying the record for the most goalscorers from any one team.

HOT STUFF FOR ROY'S BOYS

After nearly 50 years of hurt, expectations are muted about England's chances in Brazil. But even the lugubrious Roy Hodgson must have been quietly hoping for a generous draw when the balls were drawn in December 2013. Instead he got the draw from hell: testing ties against Uruguay and Costa Rica will follow an opening match against Italy in Manaus. Located in the Amazonian rain forest, with potential 99 per cent humidity and where temperatures can reach over 30 degrees, Manaus is a five-and-a-half-hour flight from England's base in

Rio. No wonder FA chairman Greg Dyke was seen to mime the slitting of his own throat when the draw was made.

SWISS CHEESED OFF

England have long been the butt of jokes about their inability to win penalty shoot-outs – but they have a long way to go to be as bad as the hapless Swiss. During a yawn-inducing goalless group match against Ukraine in 2006, Switzerland failed to score any of their three shoot-out penalties, the first team ever to do so. They also became the first team to be eliminated from the World Cup without conceding any goals. Mind you, apart from that their only defeat in 24 World Cup games, including qualifiers, was at home to Luxembourg.

A MASCOT CALLED FULECO

Following in a rich tradition of wacky mascots, the official mascot of the 2014 Fifa World Cup in Brazil is a three-banded armadillo called Fuleco. Its name is a portmanteau of the words 'Futebol' ('Football') and 'Ecologia' ('Ecology').

GERMAN HEX

England might have beaten them in 1966, but Germany/West Germany have progressed further than the three lions in each of the 10 successive tournaments, and have won the Cup twice.

THE BEST FANS IN THE WORLD?

Mexico, managed for most of their campaign by Sven-Göran Eriksson, very nearly failed to qualify for the 2010 tournament after losing three of their first four matches. This calamitous form did not stop an average of 81,600 fans watching each of their home matches – including 104,000 for the match against the USA – the highest among the finalists.

STADIUM ROUND-UP

Here's a run-down of the stadiums that will be used in the 2014 World Cup finals in Brazil.

NAME	CITY	CAPACITY	Average June /July temp
Arena de Sao Paulo	Sao Paulo	65,800	13°C–20°C
Estadio Mineirao	Belo Horizonte	62,500	25°C
Estadio Castelao	Fortaleza	64,800	30°C
Estadio do Maracana	Rio de Janeiro	76,800	25°C
Estadio Nacional	Brasilia	68,000	25°C
Arena Pernambuco	Recife	44,200	28°C
Arena Fonte Nova	Salvador	48,700	26°C
Estadio Pantanal	Cuiaba	43,000	30°C–37°C
Estadio Baixada	Curitiba	41,400	20°C
Estadio Amazonia	Manaus	42,300	30°C
Estadio das Dunas	Natal	42,000	25°C
Estadio Beira Rio	Porto Alegre	48,800	10°C–19°C

THE GROUPS

The draw for the group stage of the 2014 World Cup was made on 6 December 2013 with the following results.

GROUP A	Brazil, Croatia, Mexico, Cameroon
GROUP B	Spain, Holland, Chile, Australia
GROUP C	Colombia, Greece, Ivory Coast, Japan
GROUP D	Uruguay, Costa Rica, England, Italy
GROUP E	Switzerland, Ecuador, France, Honduras
GROUP F	Argentina, Bosnia-Herzegovina, Iran, Nigeria
GROUP G	Germany, Portugal, Ghana, USA
GROUP H	Belgium, Algeria, Russia, South Korea

Notable absentees are Russia, who lost out in the UEFA playoffs to relative minnows Slovenia, and African champions Egypt, who were defeated by Maghreb rivals Algeria in a tense playoff decider. Other national teams with considerable football pedigrees, such as Sweden, Croatia and the Czech Republic also failed to make it through the qualifying group stages.

NORTH V SOUTH CLASH AVERTED

North Korea's appearance at the 2010 World Cup was their first since 1966, and much had been made of a possible clash against South Korea in either the final or the third-place playoff. Fortunately for South East Asian harmony, the North failed to get out of their group, losing 7–0 to Portugal and 3–0 to the Ivory Coast. To their credit, their only goal came in the 89th minute of their opening match with the mighty Brazil, who had already scored twice.

FIRST PAST THE POST

The first team to qualify for the 2014 World Cup – apart from hosts Brazil, of course – was Japan when they drew 1–1 with Australia on 3 June 2013.

THE CURSE OF THE CHAMPIONS

Spain, as reigning champions, will be among the favourites in 2014. But should they be? Since Brazil's victory in 1962, no holders have ever retained the trophy.

SPICY CHILEANS

Chile amassed an impressive seven red cards during their qualifying games for the 2010 tournament – Cristian Alvarez was sent off in the first match against Argentina, then Jorge Valdivia saw red in the seventh fixture against Brazil, Ismael Fuentes and Gonzalo Jara in the ninth qualifying match against Ecuador, Mauricio Isla in the twelfth fixture against Uruguay, Alexis Sanchez in the return fixture against Brazil (Chile's sixteenth match), and then finally Fabian Orellana in the penultimate qualifying game against Colombia. Despite such a poor disciplinary record their results were good enough to ensure a second-place finish behind group winners Brazil in the CONMEBOL table, thus securing automatic qualification along with Brazil, Paraguay and Argentina. Chile shouldn't have any problems playing with 10 or even 9 men come the 2010 tournament – they are more than acquainted with it.

Strangely, in the two matches against Peru, in which a traditionally fierce rivalry dating back to the War of the Pacific often rears its ugly head, there were no Chilean sendings-off, although Peruvian winger Juan Vargas did see red, and admittedly there were 8 yellow cards dealt out in each of the home and away matches.

Chile are forever associated with the red card, it seems – apart from their nickname, la roja (the red ones), Chile legend Carlos Caszely was the first player to be officially sent off with a red card during the 1974 World Cup, in a match against West Germany.

GOALSCORING OMENS?

Germany come into the 2014 tournament as one of the European favourites on the back of having scored the most goals in qualifying, with 36. This was two more than Holland, who nevertheless had the top marksman in Robin van Persie, who scored 11 goals. England weighed in with 31 goals. In South America, Argentina top-scored with 35, with Uruguay's Luis Suarez bagging 11.

LUCKY TO BE THERE

Others got through by the skin of their teeth. They included:
ALGERIA Knocked out Burkina Faso on away goals after a 3–3 draw in their playoff tie – and had a close escape in stoppage time when a clearance struck their own crossbar.

AUSTRALIA Managed only three wins from a group containing Iraq, Oman, Jordan and Japan, form that would eventually contribute to manager Holger Osieck being sacked.

MEXICO Their defeat in the final game against Costa Rica meant Panama, playing at the same time, needed only to beat the already-qualified United States at home to book their place in Brazil. With the Panamanians leading 2–1 in injury time, the Americans struck back, scoring in the 91st and 92nd minutes, to end Panama's dream in the most painful of circumstances.

URUGUAY failed to win any of their first five away games and conceded four goals on their travels in Bolivia and Colombia, but their unbeaten home record ensured they finished fifth to book a playoff against Jordan, which they won easily.

WELCOME TO THE MODERN AGE

The 2014 World Cup finals will be the first with goal-line technology, enabling the referee to know whether a goal really is a goal.

PLAYER POOL

5,549 players attempted to qualify for the 2014 World Cup. When the eventual squads are named for next year, just 736 players will be involved from 32 teams: 96 goalkeepers and 640 outfield players.

WORLD IN MOTION

207 nations took part in the 2014 World Cup qualifiers, with Bhutan, Brunei, Guam and Mauritania opting not to compete. The first games took place on 29 June 2011, almost a full three years before the tournament proper was due to begin. Laos, Timor-Leste and Myanmar were the first teams eliminated.

SEEING RED

Savo Pavicevic of Montenegro and Aggrey Morris of Tanzania were both sent off twice during their respective countries' ultimately doomed attempts to qualify for the Brazil World Cup.

OLD AND NEW FACES

Brazil, the hosts, will be playing in their 20th straight World Cup finals when the 2014 tournament kicks off, while Italy will make their 18th appearance overall and 14th in a row. Meanwhile, Bosnia-Herzegovina will be making their first World Cup finals appearance.

BAD LUCK BAHAMAS

It may have sun and surf to die for, but you have to feel sorry for the Bahamas. Having won 4–0 and 6–0 in their double-header against the Turks and Caicos Islands to progress to Round 2 in the CONCACAF qualifying region, they were then obliged to pull out of qualifying because they couldn't provide adequate stadium facilities. They were therefore eliminated from the World Cup with a 100 per cent qualifying matches record.

LEAKY DEFENCES

San Marino did manage to score one goal in their qualifying group for Brazil 2014. Unfortunately, they also conceded 54, the worst record in the entire competition. Ukraine beat them 9–0 and England scored 8. But if it is any consolation, Liechtenstein were thumped 8–1 by Bosnia-Herzegovina, while Samoa leaked 10 against Tahiti and 9 against New Caledonia. Meanwhile Antigua and Barbuda beat US Virgin Islands 10–0 and 8–1.

DREAM TEAM

In 2002 FIFA selected their World Cup 'dream team' made up of the best players of the previous 40 years. Each to their own, of course – but Rivelino and Gerd Muller would surely have something to say about the inclusion of talented but less prolific stars Roberto Baggio and Romario.

Goalkeeper Lev Yashin (USSR)

Defenders Franz Beckenbauer (GER), Paolo Maldini (ITA), Roberto Carlos (BRA)

Midfielders Diego Maradona (ARG), Michel Platini (FRA), Zinedine Zidane (FRA), Roberto Baggio (ITA)

Forwards Johan Cruyff (HOL), Pelé (BRA), Romario (BRA)

WORLD CUP QUOTES

'The goalposts were English.'
Belgian headline after their agonising last-minute defeat by England at Italia '90.

'Up to five goals is journalism. After that, it becomes statistics.'
French reporter gives up after Sweden thrash Cuba 8–0 at the 1938 World Cup.

'God help them. Often I didn't know where the ball was going,
so how could they?'
'Der Bomber' Gerd Muller offers words of sympathy to goalkeepers.

'Home advantange is a double-edged sword; the crowd can either roar you
on, or you can crumble beneath their too-great desire, the weight of it on your
shoulders. But England didn't crumble in 1966, and 103 years after the FA was
founded in the Freemasons' Tavern in Lincoln's Inn Fields, the 8th World Cup was
played on the grounds of the world's first soccer clubs, and won and brought
home by the people who made them.'
Editorial in The Times after England won the 1966 World Cup final.

'You've won it once – now do it again.'
England boss Alf Ramsey exhorts his troops before extra time
in the 1966 World Cup final.

'It is of no purpose and it should not exist.'
French manager Michel Hidalgo dismisses the third-place playoff in 1982.

'What's to stop us beating Uruguay?'
Scotland captain Willie Cunningham on the eve of their 7–0 hiding by Uruguay
in the 1954 World Cup.

'There is only one way to describe Brazil's 1966 World Cup effort and that is to declare openly that from the beginning it was a total and unmitigated disaster. I suppose our directors put their faith in the old dictum that "God is a Brazilian" – forgetting that God also helps those who help themselves.'

The great Pelé despairs after Brazil lost to Hungary and Portugal and failed to qualify for the quarter-finals.

'Not just a defeat – a disaster!'

Headline in an Italian newspaper after the Azzurri crashed 4–0 against Switzerland in 1954.

'If I were Svensson, I wouldn't worry about this.'

Commentator Kenneth Wolstenholme with some words of consolation for the Swedish goalkeeper after Pelé had just scored a sublime goal to put Brazil 3–1 ahead in the World Cup final of 1958.

'We would have a dozen passes at our end and then try and hit the ball up to our one forward. He was bound to lose it. So they had a dozen passes down their end. It was one of the worst internationals of all time.'

Bobby Moore's verdict on England's dismal 0–0 draw against Bulgaria in Group 4 of the 1962 World Cup in Chile.

'Most unfancied teams at the World Cup at least have a puncher's chance. But the USA don't even have a puncher.'

Pundit Rodney Marsh, after the USA had been hammered 5–1 by Czechoslovakia in their opening match of the 1990 World Cup.

'No football, we're English'

Headline in *Gazzetta dello Sport* after England's turgid 1–1 draw with the Republic of Ireland in 1990. Statisticians later calculated that the ball had been in play for only 49 of the 90 minutes.

Viva World Cup!

'I would tell those gentlemen of FIFA to take their suits off and play football. If they were to think more about football and less about business there would be night games.'

Mexico coach Miguel Mejia Baron complains bitterly about FIFA's decision to play matches during the 1994 finals in the USA in the scorching midday heat in order to maximise television coverage.

'We need to shake off this Third World image. We are no more willing to see witch doctors on the pitch than cannibals at the refreshment stalls.'

A frustrated member of the African Football Confederation, after Ivory Coast had employed the services of a witch doctor prior to their World Cup qualifier against Nigeria in 1993. Ivory Coast won 2–1.

'The World Cup is like a woman. The longer you wait for one, the more you appreciate it.'

French goalkeeper Lionel Charbonnier gives his opinion on suggestions that the World Cup finals should be held every two years instead of every four.

'You are an Englishman, of course!'

West German skipper Franz Beckenbauer to referee Jack Taylor after he had just awarded Holland a second-minute penalty in the 1974 World Cup final.

'Old ladies who had been coming into my shop for years suddenly started talking to me about sweepers and creating space. That's the power of television.'

Jack Taylor, World Cup referee and Wolverhampton butcher, reflects on the fame he received after the 1974 final.

'You are pulling my trousers!'

– the reaction of a Dutch journalist after being told that Kenny Burns of Scotland's doomed 1978 World Cup squad had just been voted Player of the Year in England.